Practical Vedanta by Vivekananda

Swami Vivekananda
Institute of Thought & Philosophy

GRAPEVINE INDIA

Published by

GRAPEVINE INDIA PUBLISHERS PVT LTD

www.grapevineindia.com
Delhi | Mumbai
email: grapevineindiapublishers@gmail.com

Ordering Information:
Quantity sales: Special discounts are available on quantity purchases by corporations, associations, and others.
For details, reach out to the publisher.

First published by Grapevine India 2024

The mission of the Institute of Thought and Philosophy is to preserve and propagate the teachings of Swami Vivekananda. This great Indian spiritual leader is known for introducing the West to Hinduism. Drawing from his vast literary legacy, we provide valuable insights and practical guidance for modern living.

Have any query or feedback? Please reach out to us at
ITPPress123@gmail.com

Practical Vedanta: Part 1

(Delivered in London, 10th November 1896)

I have been asked to say something about the practical position of the Vedanta philosophy. As I have told you, theory is very good indeed, but how are we to carry it into practice? If it be absolutely impracticable, no theory is of any value whatever, except as intellectual gymnastics. The Vedanta, therefore, as a religion must be intensely practical. We must be able to carry it out in every part of our lives. And not only this, the fictitious differentiation between religion and the life of the world must vanish, for the Vedanta teaches oneness — one life throughout. The ideals of religion must cover the whole field of life, they must enter into all our thoughts, and more and more into practice. I will enter gradually on the practical side as we proceed. But this series of lectures is intended to be a basis, and so we must first apply ourselves to theories and understand how they are worked out, proceeding from forest caves to busy streets and cities; and one peculiar feature we find is that many of these thoughts have been the outcome, not of retirement into forests, but have emanated from persons whom we expect to lead the busiest lives — from ruling monarchs.

Shvetaketu was the son of Âruni, a sage, most probably a recluse. He was brought up in the forest, but he went to the city of the Panchâlas and appeared at the court of the king, Pravâhana Jaivali. The king asked him, "Do you know how beings depart hence at death?" "No, sir." "Do you know how they return hither?" "No, sir." "Do you know the way of the fathers and the way of the gods?" "No, sir." Then the king asked other questions. Shvetaketu could not answer them. So the king told him that he knew nothing. The boy went back to his father, and the father admitted that he himself could not answer these questions. It was not that he was unwilling to answer these questions. It was not that he was unwilling to teach the boy, but he did not know these things. So he went to the king and asked to be taught these secrets. The king said that these things had been hitherto known only among kings; the priests never knew them. He, however, proceeded to teach him what he desired to know. In various Upanishads we find that this Vedanta philosophy is not the outcome of meditation in the forests only, but that the very best parts of it were thought out and expressed by brains which were busiest in the everyday affairs of life. We cannot conceive any man busier than an absolute monarch, a man who is ruling over millions of people, and yet, some of these rulers were deep thinkers.

Everything goes to show that this philosophy must be very practical; and later on, when we come to the Bhagavad-Gita — most of you, perhaps, have read it, it is the best commentary we have on the Vedanta philosophy — curiously enough the scene is laid on the battlefield, where Krishna teaches this philosophy to Arjuna; and the doctrine which stands out luminously in every page of the Gita is intense activity, but in the midst of it, eternal calmness. This is the secret of work, to attain which is the goal of the Vedanta. Inactivity, as we understand it in the sense of passivity, certainly cannot be the goal. Were it so, then the walls around us would be the most intelligent; they are inactive. Clods of earth, stumps of trees, would be the greatest sages in the world; they are inactive. Nor does inactivity become activity when it is combined with passion. Real activity, which is the goal of Vedanta, is combined with eternal calmness, the calmness which cannot be ruffled, the balance of mind which is never disturbed, whatever happens. And we all know from our experience in life that that is the best attitude for work.

I have been asked many times how we can work if we do not have the passion which we generally feel for work. I also thought in that way years ago, but as I am growing older, getting more experience, I find it is not true. The less passion there is, the better we work. The calmer we are, the better for us, and the more the amount of work we can do. When we let loose our feelings, we waste so much energy, shatter our nerves, disturb our minds, and accomplish very little work. The energy which ought to have gone out as work is spent as mere feeling, which counts for nothing. It is only when the mind is very calm and collected that the whole of its energy is spent in doing good work. And if you read the lives of the great workers which the world has produced, you will find that they were wonderfully calm men. Nothing, as it were, could throw them off their balance. That is why the man who becomes angry never does a great amount of work, and the man whom nothing can make angry accomplishes so much. The man who gives way to anger, or hatred, or any other passion, cannot work; he only breaks himself to pieces, and does nothing practical. It is the calm, forgiving, equable, well-balanced mind that does the greatest amount of work.

The Vedanta preaches the ideal; and the ideal, as we know, is always far ahead of the real, of the practical, as we may call it. There are two tendencies in human nature: one to harmonise the ideal with the life, and the other to elevate the life to the ideal. It is a great thing to understand this, for the former tendency is the temptation of our lives. I think that I can only do a certain class of work. Most of it, perhaps, is bad; most of it, perhaps, has a motive power of passion behind it, anger, or greed, or selfishness. Now if any man comes to preach to me a certain ideal, the first step towards which is to give up selfishness, to give up self-enjoyment, I think that is impractical. But when a man brings an ideal which can be reconciled with my selfishness, I am glad at once and jump at it. That is the ideal for me. As the word "orthodox" has been manipulated into various forms, so has been the word "practical". "My doxy is orthodoxy; your doxy is heterodoxy." So with practicality. What I think is practical, is to me the only practicality in the world. If I am a shopkeeper, I think shopkeeping the only practical pursuit in the world. If I am a thief, I think stealing is the best means of being practical; others are not practical. You see how we all use this word practical for things we like and can do. Therefore I will ask you to understand that Vedanta, though it is intensely practical, is always so in the sense of the ideal. It does not preach an impossible ideal, however high it be, and it is high enough for an ideal. In one word, this ideal is that you are divine, "Thou art That". This is the essence of Vedanta; after all its ramifications and intellectual gymnastics, you know the human soul to be pure and omniscient, you see that such superstitions as birth and death would be entire nonsense when spoken of in connection with the soul. The soul was never born and will never die, and all these ideas that we are going to die and are afraid to die are mere superstitions. And all such ideas as that we can do this or cannot do that are superstitions. We can do everything. The Vedanta teaches men to have faith in themselves first. As certain religions of the world say that a man who does not believe in a Personal God outside of himself is an atheist, so the Vedanta says, a man who does not believe in himself is an atheist. Not believing in the glory of our own soul is what the Vedanta calls atheism. To many this is, no doubt, a terrible idea; and most of us think that this ideal can never be reached; but the Vedanta insists that it can be realised by every one. There is neither man nor woman or child, nor difference of race or sex, nor anything that stands as a bar to the realisation of the ideal, because Vedanta shows that it is realised already, it is already there.

All the powers in the universe are already ours. It is we who have put our hands before our eyes and cry that it is dark. Know that there is no darkness around us. Take the hands away and there is the light which was from the beginning. Darkness never existed, weakness never existed. We who are fools cry that we are weak; we who are fools cry that we are impure. Thus Vedanta not only insists that the ideal is practical, but that it has been so all the time; and this Ideal, this Reality, is our own nature. Everything else that you see is false, untrue. As soon as you say, "I am a little mortal being," you are saying something which is not true, you are giving the lie to yourselves, you are hypnotising yourselves into something vile and weak and wretched.

The Vedanta recognises no sin, it only recognises error. And the greatest error, says the Vedanta, is to say that you are weak, that you are a sinner, a miserable creature, and that you have no power and you cannot do this and that.

Every time you think in that way, you, as it were, rivet one more link in the chain that binds you down, you add one more layer of hypnotism on to your own soul. Therefore, whosoever thinks he is weak is wrong, whosoever thinks he is impure is wrong, and is throwing a bad thought into the world. This we must always bear in mind that in the Vedanta there is no attempt at reconciling the present life — the hypnotised life, this false life which we have assumed — with the ideal; but this false life must go, and the real life which is always existing must manifest itself, must shine out. No man becomes purer and purer, it is a matter of greater manifestation. The veil drops away, and the native purity of the soul begins to manifest itself. Everything is ours already — infinite purity, freedom, love, and power.

The Vedanta also says that not only can this be realised in the depths of forests or caves, but by men in all possible conditions of life. We have seen that the people who discovered these truths were neither living in caves nor forests, nor following the ordinary vocations of life, but men who, we have every reason to believe, led the busiest of lives, men who had to command armies, to sit on thrones, and look to the welfare of millions — and all these, in the days of absolute monarchy, and not as in these days when a king is to a great extent a mere figurehead. Yet they could find time to think out all these thoughts, to realise them, and to teach them to humanity. How much more then should it be practical for us whose lives, compared with theirs, are lives of leisure? That we cannot realise them is a shame to us, seeing that we are comparatively free all the time, having very little to do. My requirements are as nothing compared with those of an ancient absolute monarch. My wants are as nothing compared with the demands of Arjuna on the battlefield of Kurukshetra, commanding a huge army; and yet he could find time in the midst of the din and turmoil of battle to talk the highest philosophy and to carry it into his life also. Surely we ought to be able to do as much in this life of ours — comparatively free, easy, and comfortable. Most of us here have more time than we think we have, if we really want to use it for good. With the amount of freedom we have we can attain to two hundred ideals in this life, if we will, but we must not degrade the ideal to the actual. One of the most insinuating things comes to us in the shape of persons who apologise for our mistakes and teach us how to make special excuses for all our foolish wants and foolish desires; and we think that their ideal is the only ideal we need have. But it is not so. The Vedanta teaches no such thing. The actual should be reconciled to the ideal, the present life should be made to coincide with life eternal.

For you must always remember that the one central ideal of Vedanta is this oneness. There are no two in anything, no two lives, nor even two different kinds of life for the two worlds. You will find the Vedas speaking of heavens and things like that at first; but later on, when they come to the highest ideals of their philosophy, they brush away all these things. There is but one life, one world, one existence. Everything is that One, the difference is in degree and not in kind. The difference between our lives is not in kind. The Vedanta entirely denies such ideas as that animals are separate from men, and that they were made and created by God to be used for our food.

Some people have been kind enough to start an antivivisection society. I asked a member, "Why do you think, my friend, that it is quite lawful to kill animals for food, and not to kill one or two for scientific experiments?" He replied, "Vivisection is most horrible, but animals have been given to us for food." Oneness includes all animals. If man's life is immortal, so also is the animal's. The difference is only in degree and not in kind. The amoeba and I are the same, the difference is only in degree; and from the standpoint of the highest life, all these differences vanish. A man may see a great deal of difference between grass and a little tree, but if you mount very high, the grass and the biggest tree will appear much the same. So, from the standpoint of the highest ideal, the lowest animal and the highest man are the same. If you believe there is a God, the animals and the highest creatures must be the same. A God who is partial to his children called men, and cruel to his children called brute beasts, is worse than a demon. I would rather die a hundred times than worship such a God. My whole life would be a fight with such a God But there is no difference, and those who say there is, are irresponsible, heartless people who do not know. Here is a case of the word practical used in a wrong sense. I myself may not be a very strict vegetarian, but I understand the ideal. When I eat meat I know it is wrong. Even if I am bound to eat it under certain circumstances, I know it is cruel. I must not drag my ideal down to the actual and apologise for my weak conduct in this way. The ideal is not to eat flesh, not to injure any being, for all animals are my brothers. If you can think of them as your brothers, you have made a little headway towards the brotherhood of all souls, not to speak of the brotherhood of man! That is child's play. You generally find that this is not very acceptable to many, because it teaches them to give up the actual, and go higher up to the ideal. But if you bring out a theory which is reconciled with their present conduct, they regard it as entirely practical.

There is this strongly conservative tendency in human nature: we do not like to move one step forward. I think of mankind just as I read of persons who become frozen in snow; all such, they say, want to go to sleep, and if you try to drag them up, they say, "Let me sleep; it is so beautiful to sleep in the snow", and they die there in that sleep. So is our nature. That is what we are doing all our life, getting frozen from the feet upwards, and yet wanting to sleep. Therefore you must struggle towards the ideal, and if a man comes who wants to bring that ideal down to your level, and teach a religion that does not carry that highest ideal, do not listen to him. To me that is an impracticable religion. But if a man teaches a religion which presents the highest ideal, I am ready for him. Beware when anyone is trying to apologise for sense vanities and sense weaknesses. If anyone wants to preach that way to us, poor, sense-bound clods of earth as we have made ourselves by following that teaching, we shall never progress. I have seen many of these things, have had some experience of the world, and my country is the land where religious sects grow like mushrooms. Every year new sects arise. But one thing I have marked, that it is only those that never want to reconcile the man of flesh with the man of truth that make progress. Wherever there is this false idea of reconciling fleshly vanities with the highest ideals, of dragging down God to the level of man, there comes decay. Man should not be degraded to worldly slavery, but should be raised up to God.

At the same time, there is another side to the question. We must not look down with contempt on others. All of us are going towards the same goal. The difference between weakness and strength is one of degree; the difference between virtue and vice is one of degree, the difference between heaven and hell is one of degree, the difference between life and death is one of degree, all differences in this world are of degree, and not of kind, because oneness is the secret of everything. All is One, which manifests Itself, either as thought, or life, or soul, or body, and the difference is only in degree. As such, we have no right to look down with contempt upon those who are not developed exactly in the same degree as we are. Condemn none; if you can stretch out a helping hand, do so. If you cannot, fold your hands, bless your brothers, and let them go their own way. Dragging down and condemning is not the way to work. Never is work accomplished in that way. We spend our energies in condemning others. Criticism and condemnation is a vain way of spending our energies, for in the long run we come to learn that all are seeing the same thing, are more or less approaching the same ideal, and that most of our differences are merely differences of expression.

Take the idea of sin. I was telling you just now the Vedantic idea of it, and the other idea is that man is a sinner. They are practically the same, only the one takes the positive and the other the negative side. One shows to man his strength and the other his weakness. There may be weakness, says the Vedanta, but never mind, we want to grow. Disease was found out as soon as man was born. Everyone knows his disease; it requires no one to tell us what our diseases are. But thinking all the time that we are diseased will not cure us — medicine is necessary. We may forget anything outside, we may try to become hypocrites to the external world, but in our heart of hearts we all know our weaknesses. But, says the Vedanta, being reminded of weakness does not help much; give strength, and strength does not come by thinking of weakness all the time. The remedy for weakness is not brooding over weakness, but thinking of strength. Teach men of the strength that is already within them. Instead of telling them they are sinners, the Vedanta takes the opposite position, and says, "You are pure and perfect, and what you call sin does not belong to you." Sins are very low degrees of Self-manifestation; manifest your Self in a high degree. That is the one thing to remember; all of us can do that. Never say, "No", never say, "I cannot", for you are infinite. Even time and space are as nothing compared with your nature. You can do anything and everything, you are almighty.

These are the principles of ethics, but we shall now come down lower and work out the details. We shall see how this Vedanta can be carried into our everyday life, the city life, the country life, the national life, and the home life of every nation. For, if a religion cannot help man wherever he may be, wherever he stands, it is not of much use; it will remain only a theory for the chosen few. Religion, to help mankind, must be ready and able to help him in whatever condition he is, in servitude or in freedom, in the depths of degradation or on the heights of purity; everywhere, equally, it should be able to come to his aid. The principles of Vedanta, or the ideal of religion, or whatever you may call it, will be fulfilled by its capacity for performing this great function.

The ideal of faith in ourselves is of the greatest help to us. If faith in ourselves had been more extensively taught and practiced, I am sure a very large portion of the evils and miseries that we have would have vanished. Throughout the history of mankind, if any motive power has been more potent than another in the lives of all great men and women, it is that of faith in themselves. Born with the consciousness that they were to be great, they became great. Let a man go down as low as possible; there must come a time when out of sheer desperation he will take an upward curve and will learn to have faith in himself. But it is better for us that we should know it from the very first. Why should we have all these bitter experiences in order to gain faith in ourselves? We can see that all the difference between man and man is owing to the existence or non-existence of faith in himself. Faith in ourselves will do everything. I have experienced it in my own life, and am still doing so; and as I grow older that faith is becoming stronger and stronger. He is an atheist who does not believe in himself. The old religions said that he was an atheist who did not believe in God. The new religion says that he is the atheist who does not believe in himself. But it is not selfish faith because the Vedanta, again, is the doctrine of oneness. It means faith in all, because you are all. Love for yourselves means love for all, love for animals, love for everything, for you are all one. It is the great faith which will make the world better. I am sure of that. He is the highest man who can say with truth, "I know all about myself." Do you know how much energy, how many powers, how many forces are still lurking behind that frame of yours? What scientist has known all that is in man? Millions of years have passed since man first came here, and yet but one infinitesimal part of his powers has been manifested. Therefore, you must not say that you are weak. How do you know what possibilities lie behind that degradation on the surface? You know but little of that which is within you. For behind you is the ocean of infinite power and blessedness.

"This Âtman is first to be heard of." Hear day and night that you are that Soul. Repeat it to yourselves day and night till it enters into your very veins, till it tingles in every drop of blood, till it is in your flesh and bone. Let the whole body be full of that one ideal, "I am the birthless, the deathless, the blissful, the omniscient, the omnipotent, ever-glorious Soul." Think on it day and night; think on it till it becomes part and parcel of your life. Meditate upon it, and out of that will come work. "Out of the fullness of the heart the mouth speaketh," and out of the fullness of the heart the hand worketh also. Action will come. Fill yourselves with the ideal; whatever you do, think well on it. All your actions will be magnified, transformed, deified, by the very power of the thought. If matter is powerful, thought is omnipotent. Bring this thought to bear upon your life, fill yourselves with the thought of your almightiness, your majesty, and your glory. Would to God no superstitions had been put into your head! Would to God we had not been surrounded from our birth by all these superstitious influences and paralysing ideas of our weakness and vileness! Would to God that mankind had had an easier path through which to attain to the noblest and highest truths! But man had to pass through all this; do not make the path more difficult for those who are coming after you.

These are sometimes terrible doctrines to teach. I know people who get frightened at these ideas, but for those who want to be practical, this is the first thing to learn. Never tell yourselves or others that you are weak. Do good if you can, but do not injure the world. You know in your inmost heart that many of your limited ideas,

this humbling of yourself and praying and weeping to imaginary beings are superstitions. Tell me one case where these prayers have been answered. All the answers that came were from your own hearts. You know there are no ghosts, but no sooner are you in the dark than you feel a little creepy sensation. That is so because in our childhood we have had all these fearful ideas put into our heads. But do not teach these things to others through fear of society and public opinion, through fear of incurring the hatred of friends, or for fear of losing cherished superstitions. Be masters of all these. What is there to be taught more in religion than the oneness of the universe and faith in one's self? All the works of mankind for thousands of years past have been towards this one goal, and mankind is yet working it out. It is your turn now and you already know the truth. For it has been taught on all sides. Not only philosophy and psychology, but materialistic sciences have declared it. Where is the scientific man today who fears to acknowledge the truth of this oneness of the universe? Who is there who dares talk of many worlds? All these are superstitions. There is only one life and one world, and this one life and one world is appearing to us as manifold. This manifoldness is like a dream. When you dream, one dream passes away and another comes. You do not live in your dreams. The dreams come one after another, scene after scene unfolds before you. So it is in this world of ninety per cent misery and ten per cent happiness. Perhaps after a while it will appear as ninety per cent happiness, and we shall call it heaven, but a time comes to the sage when the whole thing vanishes, and this world appears as God Himself, and his own soul as God. It is not therefore that there are many worlds, it is not that there are many lives. All this manifoldness is the manifestation of that One. That One is manifesting Himself as many, as matter, spirit, mind, thought, and everything else. It is that One, manifesting Himself as many. Therefore the first step for us to take is to teach the truth to ourselves and to others.

Let the world resound with this ideal, and let superstitions vanish. Tell it to men who are weak and persist in telling it. You are the Pure One; awake and arise, O mighty one, this sleep does not become you. Awake and arise, it does not befit you. Think not that you are weak and miserable. Almighty, arise and awake, and manifest your own nature. It is not fitting that you think yourself a sinner. It is not fitting that you think yourself weak. Say that to the world, say it to yourselves, and see what a practical result comes, see how with an electric flash everything is manifested, how everything is changed. Tell that to mankind, and show them their power. Then we shall learn how to apply it in our daily lives.

To be able to use what we call Viveka (discrimination), to learn how in every moment of our lives, in every one of our actions, to discriminate between what is right and wrong, true and false, we shall have to know the test of truth, which is purity, oneness. Everything that makes for oneness is truth. Love is truth, and hatred is false, because hatred makes for multiplicity. It is hatred that separates man from man; therefore it is wrong and false. It is a disintegrating power; it separates and destroys.

Love binds, love makes for that oneness. You become one, the mother with the child, families with the city, the whole world becomes one with the animals. For love is Existence, God Himself; and all this is the manifestation of that One Love, more or less expressed. The difference is only in degree, but it is the manifestation of that One

Love throughout. Therefore in all our actions we have to judge whether it is making for diversity or for oneness. If for diversity we have to give it up, but if it makes for oneness we are sure it is good. So with our thoughts; we have to decide whether they make for disintegration, multiplicity, or for oneness, binding soul to soul and bringing one influence to bear. If they do this, we will take them up, and if not, we will throw them off as criminal.

The whole idea of ethics is that it does not depend on anything unknowable, it does not teach anything unknown, but in the language of the Upanishad, "The God whom you worship as an unknown God, the same I preach unto thee." It is through the Self that you know anything. I see the chair; but to see the chair, I have first to perceive myself and then the chair. It is in and through the Self that the chair is perceived. It is in and through the Self that you are known to me, that the whole world is known to me; and therefore to say this Self is unknown is sheer nonsense. Take off the Self and the whole universe vanishes. In and through the Self all knowledge comes. Therefore it is the best known of all. It is yourself, that which you call I. You may wonder how this I of me can be the I of you. You may wonder how this limited I can be the unlimited Infinite, but it is so. The limited is a mere fiction. The Infinite has been covered up, as it were, and a little of It is manifesting as the I. Limitation can never come upon the unlimited; it is a fiction. The Self is known, therefore, to every one of us — man, woman, or child — and even to animals. Without knowing Him we can neither live nor move, nor have our being; without knowing this Lord of all, we cannot breathe or live a second. The God of the Vedanta is the most known of all and is not the outcome of imagination.

If this is not preaching a practical God, how else could you teach a practical God? Where is there a more practical God than He whom I see before me — a God omnipresent, in every being, more real than our senses? For you are He, the Omnipresent God Almighty, the Soul of your souls, and if I say you are not, I tell an untruth. I know it, whether at all times I realise it or not. He is the Oneness, the Unity of all, the Reality of all life and all existence.

These ideas of the ethics of Vedanta have to be worked out in detail, and, therefore, you must have patience. As I have told you, we want to take the subject in detail and work it up thoroughly, to see how the ideas grow from very low ideals, and how the one great Ideal of oneness has developed and become shaped into the universal love; and we ought to study these in order to avoid dangers. The world cannot find time to work it up from the lowest steps. But what is the use of our standing on higher steps if we cannot give the truth to others coming afterwards? Therefore, it is better to study it in all its workings; and first, it is absolutely necessary to clear the intellectual portion, although we know that intellectuality is almost nothing; for it is the heart that is of most importance. It is through the heart that the Lord is seen, and not through the intellect. The intellect is only the street-cleaner, cleansing the path for us, a secondary worker, the policeman; but the policeman is not a positive necessity for the workings of society. He is only to stop disturbances, to check wrong-doing, and that is all the work required of the intellect. When you read intellectual books, you think when you have mastered them, "Bless the Lord that I am out of them", because the intellect is blind and cannot move of itself, it has neither hands nor feet. It is feeling that works, that moves with speed infinitely superior to that of electricity or anything else. Do you feel? — that is the question. If you do, you will see the Lord: It is the feeling that you have today that will be intensified, deified, raised to the highest platform, until it feels everything, the oneness in everything, till it feels God in itself and in others. The intellect can never do that. "Different methods of speaking words, different methods of explaining the texts of books, these are for the enjoyment of the learned, not for the salvation of the soul" (Vivekachudâmani, 58).

Those of you who have read Thomas a Kempis know how in every page he insists on this, and almost every holy man in the world has insisted on it. Intellect is necessary, for without it we fall into crude errors and make all sorts of mistakes. Intellect checks these; but beyond that, do not try to build anything upon it. It is an inactive, secondary help; the real help is feeling, love. Do you feel for others? If you do, you are growing in oneness. If you do not feel for others, you may be the most intellectual giant ever born, but you will be nothing; you are but dry intellect, and you will remain so. And if you feel, even if you cannot read any book and do not know any language, you are in the right way. The Lord is yours.

Do you not know from the history of the world where the power of the prophets lay? Where was it? In the intellect? Did any of them write a fine book on philosophy, on the most intricate ratiocinations of logic? Not one of them. They only spoke a few words. Feel like Christ and you will be a Christ; feel like Buddha and you will be a Buddha. It is feeling that is the life, the strength, the

vitality, without which no amount of intellectual activity can reach God. Intellect is like limbs without the power of locomotion. It is only when feeling enters and gives them motion that they move and work on others. That is so all over the world, and it is a thing which you must always remember. It is one of the most practical things in Vedantic morality, for it is the teaching of the Vedanta that you are all prophets, and all must be prophets. The book is not the proof of your conduct, but you are the proof of the book. How do you know that a book teaches truth? Because you are truth and feel it. That is what the Vedanta says. What is the proof of the Christs and Buddhas of the world? That you and I feel like them. That is how you and I understand that they were true. Our prophet-soul is the proof of their prophet-soul. Your godhead is the proof of God Himself. If you are not a prophet, there never has been anything true of God. If you are not God, there never was any God, and never will be. This, says the Vedanta, is the ideal to follow. Every one of us will have to become a prophet, and you are that already. Only know it. Never think there is anything impossible for the soul. It is the greatest heresy to think so. If there is sin, this is the only sin — to say that you are weak, or others are weak.

Practical Vedanta: Part 2

(Delivered in London, 12th November 1896)

I will relate to you a very ancient story from the Chhândogya Upanishad, which tells how knowledge came to a boy. The form of the story is very crude, but we shall find that it contains a principle. A young boy said to his mother, "I am going to study the Vedas. Tell me the name of my father and my caste." The mother was not a married woman, and in India the child of a woman who has not been married is considered an outcast; he is not recognised by society and is not entitled to study the Vedas. So the poor mother said, "My child, I do not know your family name; I was in service, and served in different places; I do not know who your father is, but my name is Jabâlâ and your name is Satyakâma." The little child went to a sage and asked to be taken as a student. The sage asked him, "What is the name of your father, and what is your caste?" The boy repeated to him what he had heard from his mother. The sage at once said, "None but a Brâhmin could speak such a damaging truth about himself. You are a Brahmin and I will teach you. You have not swerved from truth." So he kept the boy with him and educated him.

Now come some of the peculiar methods of education in ancient India. This teacher gave Satyakama four hundred lean, weak cows to take care of, and sent him to the forest. There he went and lived for some time. The teacher had told him to come back when the herd would increase to the number of one thousand. After a few years, one day

Satyakama heard a big bull in the herd saying to him, "We are a thousand now; take us back to your teacher. I will teach you a little of Brahman." "Say on, sir," said Satyakama. Then the bull said, "The East is a part of the Lord, so is the West, so is the South, so is the North. The four cardinal points are the four parts of Brahman. Fire will also teach you something of Brahman." Fire was a great symbol in those days, and every student had to procure fire and make offerings. So on the following day, Satyakama started for his Guru's house, and when in the evening he had performed his oblation, and worshipped at the fire, and was sitting near it, he heard a voice come from the fire, "O Satyakama." "Speak, Lord," said Satyakama. (Perhaps you may remember a very similar story in the Old Testament, how Samuel heard a mysterious voice.) "O Satyakama, I am come to teach you a little of Brahman. This earth is a portion of that Brahman. The sky and the heaven are portions of It. The ocean is a part of that Brahman." Then the fire said that a certain bird would also teach him something. Satyakama continued his journey and on the next day when he had performed his evening sacrifice a swan came to him and said, "I will teach you something about Brahman. This fire which you worship, O Satyakama, is a part of that Brahman. The sun is a part, the moon is a part, the lightning is a part of that Brahman. A bird called Madgu will tell you more about it." The next evening that bird came, and a similar voice was heard by Satyakama, "I will tell you something about Brahman. Breath is a part of Brahman, sight is a part, hearing is a part, the mind is a part." Then the boy arrived at his teacher's place and presented himself before him with due reverence. No sooner had the teacher seen this disciple than he remarked: "Satyakama, thy face shines like that of a knower of Brahman! Who then has taught thee?" "Beings other than men," replied Satyakama. "But I wish that you should teach me, sir. For I have heard from men like you that knowledge which is learnt from a Guru alone leads to the supreme good." Then the sage taught him the same knowledge which he had received from the gods. "And nothing was left out, yea, nothing was left out."

Now, apart from the allegories of what the bull, the fire, and the birds taught, we see the tendency of the thought and the direction in which it was going in those days. The great idea of which we here see the germ is that all these voices are inside ourselves. As we understand these truths better, we find that the voice is in our own heart, and the student understood that all the time he was hearing the truth; but his explanation was not correct. He was interpreting the voice as coming from the external world, while all the time, it was within him. The second idea that we get is that of making the knowledge of the Brahman practical. The world is always seeking the practical possibilities of religion, and we find in these stories how it was becoming more and more practical every day. The truth was shown through everything with which the students were familiar. The fire they were worshipping was Brahman, the earth was a part of Brahman, and so on.

The next story belongs to Upakosala Kâmalâyana, a disciple of this Satyakama, who went to be taught by him and dwelt with him for some time. Now Satyakama went away on a journey, and the student became very downhearted; and when the teacher's wife came and asked him why he was not eating, the boy said, "I am too unhappy to eat." Then a voice came from the fire he was worshipping, saying "This life is Brahman, Brahman is the ether, and Brahman is happiness. Know Brahman." "I know, sir," the boy replied, "that life is Brahman, but that It is ether and happiness I do not

know." Then it explained that the two words ether and happiness signified one thing in reality, viz. the sentient ether (pure intelligence) that resides in the heart. So, it taught him Brahman as life and as the ether in the heart. Then the fire taught him, "This earth, food, fire, and sun whom you worship, are forms of Brahman. The person that is seen in the sun, I am He. He who knows this and meditates on Him, all his sins vanish and he has long life and becomes happy. He who lives in the cardinal points, the moon, the stars, and the water, I am He. He who lives in this life, the ether, the heavens, and the lightning, I am He." Here too we see the same idea of practical religion. The things which they were worshipping, such as the fire, the sun, the moon, and so forth, and the voice with which they were familiar, form the subject of the stories which explain them and give them a higher meaning. And this is the real, practical side of Vedanta. It does not destroy the world, but it explains it; it does not destroy the person, but explains him; it does not destroy the individuality, but explains it by showing the real individuality. It does not show that this world is vain and does not exist, but it says, "Understand what this world is, so that it may not hurt you." The voice did not say to Upakosala that the fire which he was worshipping, or the sun, or the moon, or the lightning, or anything else, was all wrong, but it showed him that the same spirit which was inside the sun, and moon, and lightning, and the fire, and the earth, was in him, so that everything became transformed, as it were, in the eyes of Upakosala. The fire which was merely a material fire before, in which to make oblations, assumed a new aspect and became the Lord. The earth became transformed, life became transformed, the sun, the moon, the stars, the lightning, everything became transformed and deified. Their real nature was known. The theme of the Vedanta is to see the Lord in everything, to see things in their real nature, not as they appear to be. Then another lesson is taught in the Upanishads: "He who shines through the eyes is Brahman; He is the Beautiful One, He is the Shining One. He shines in all these worlds." A certain peculiar light, a commentator says, which comes to the pure man, is what is meant by the light in the eyes, and it is said that when a man is pure such a light will shine in his eyes, and that light belongs really to the Soul within, which is everywhere. It is the same light which shines in the planets, in the stars, and suns.

I will now read to you some other doctrine of these ancient Upanishads, about birth and death and so on. Perhaps it will interest you. Shvetaketu went to the king of the Panchâlas, and the king asked him, "Do you know where people go when they die? Do you know how they come back? Do you know why the other world does not become full?" The boy replied that he did not know. Then he went to his father and asked him the same questions. The father said, "I do not know," and he went to the king. The king said that this knowledge was never known to the priests, it was only with the kings, and that was the reason why kings ruled the world. This man stayed with the king for some time, for the king said he would teach him. "The other world, O Gautama, is the fire. The sun is its fuel. The rays are the smoke. The day is the flame. The moon is the embers. And the stars are the sparks. In this fire the gods pour libation of faith and from this libation king Soma is born." So on he goes. "You need not make oblation to that little fire: the whole world is that fire, and this oblation, this worship, is continually going on. The gods, and the angels, and everybody is worshipping it. Man is the greatest symbol of fire, the body of man." Here also we see the ideal becoming practical and Brahman is seen in everything. The principle that underlies all these stories is that invented symbolism may be good and helpful, but already better symbols exist than any we can invent. You may invent an image through which to worship God, but a better image already exists, the living man. You may build a temple in which to worship God, and that may be good, but a better one, a much higher one, already exists, the human body.

You remember that the Vedas have two parts, the ceremonial and the knowledge portions. In time ceremonials had multiplied and become so intricate that it was almost hopeless to disentangle them, and so in the Upanishads we find that the ceremonials are almost done away with, but gently, by explaining them. We see that in old times they had these oblations and sacrifices, then the philosophers came, and instead of snatching away the symbols from the hands of the ignorant, instead of taking the negative position, which we unfortunately find so general in modern reforms, they gave them something to take their place. "Here is the symbol of fire," they said. "Very good! But here is another symbol, the earth. What a grand, great symbol! Here is this little temple, but the whole universe is a temple; a man can worship anywhere. There are the peculiar figures that men draw on the earth, and there are the altars, but here is the greatest of altars, the living, conscious human body, and to worship at this altar is far higher than the worship of any dead symbols."

We now come to a peculiar doctrine. I do not understand much of it myself. If you can make something out of it, I will read it to you. When a man dies, who has by meditation purified himself and got knowledge, he first goes to light, then from light to day, from day to the light half of the moon, from that to the six months when the sun goes to the north, from that to the year, from the year to the sun, from the sun to the moon, from the moon to the lightning, and when he comes to the sphere of lightning, he meets a person who is not human, and that person leads him to (the conditioned) Brahman. This is the way of the gods. When sages and wise persons die, they go that way and they do not return. What is meant by this month and year, and all these things, no one understands clearly. Each one gives his own meaning, and some say it is all nonsense. What is meant by going to the world of the moon and of the sun, and this person who comes to help the soul after it has reached the sphere of lightning, no one knows. There is an idea among the Hindus that the moon is a place where life exists, and we shall see how life has come from there. Those that have not attained to knowledge, but have done good work in this life, first go, when they die, through smoke, then to night, then to the dark fifteen days, then to the six months when the sun goes to the south, and from that they go to the region of their forefathers, then to ether, then to the region of the moon, and there become the food of the gods, and later, are born as gods and live there so long as their good works will permit. And when the effect of the good work has been finished, they come back to earth by the same route. They first become ether, and then air, and then smoke, and then mist, then cloud, and then fall upon the earth as raindrops; then they get into food, which is eaten up by human beings, and finally become their children. Those whose works have been very good take birth in good families, and those whose works have been bad take bad births, even in animal bodies. Animals are continually coming to and going from this earth. That is why the earth is neither full nor empty.

Several ideas we can get also from this, and later on, perhaps, we shall be able to understand it better, and we can speculate a little upon what it means. The last part which deals with how those who have been in heaven return, is clearer, perhaps, than the first part; but the whole idea seems to be this that there is no permanent heaven without realising God. Now some people who have not realised God, but have done good work in this world, with the view of enjoying the results, go, when they die, through this and that place, until they reach heaven, and there they are born in the same way as we are here, as children of the gods, and they live there as long as their good works will permit. Out of this comes one basic idea of the Vedanta that everything which has name and form is transient. This earth is transient, because it has name and form, and so the heavens must be transient, because there also name and form remain. A heaven which is eternal will be contradictory in terms, because everything that has name and form must begin in time, exist in time, and end in time. These are settled doctrines of the Vedanta, and as such the heavens are given up.

We have seen in the Samhitâ that the idea of heaven was that it was eternal, much the same as is prevalent among Mohammedans and Christians. The Mohammedans concretise it a little more. They say it is a place where there are gardens, beneath which rivers run. In the desert of Arabia water is very desirable, so the Mohammedan always conceives of his heaven as containing much water. I was born in a country where there are six months of rain every year. I should think of heaven, I suppose, as a dry place, and so also would the English people. These heavens in the Samhita are eternal, and the departed have beautiful bodies and live with their

forefathers, and are happy ever afterwards. There they meet with their parents, children, and other relatives, and lead very much the same sort of life as here, only much happier. All the difficulties and obstructions to happiness in this life have vanished, and only its good parts and enjoyments remain. But however comfortable mankind may consider this state of things, truth is one thing and comfort is another. There are cases where truth is not comfortable until we reach its climax. Human nature is very conservative It does something, and having once done that, finds it hard to get out of it. The mind will not receive new thoughts, because they bring discomfort.

In the Upanishads, we see a tremendous departure made. It is declared that these heavens in which men live with the ancestors after death cannot be permanent, seeing that everything which has name and form must die. If there are heavens with forms, these heavens must vanish in course of time; they may last millions of years, but there must come a time when they will have to go. With this idea came another that these souls must come back to earth, and that heavens are places where they enjoy the results of their good works, and after these effects are finished they come back into this earth life again. One thing is clear from this that mankind had a perception of the philosophy of causation even at the early time. Later on we shall see how our philosophers bring that out in the language of philosophy and logic, but here it is almost in the language of children. One thing you may remark in reading these books that it is all internal perception. If you ask me if this can be practical, my answer is, it has been practical first, and philosophical next. You can see that first these things have been perceived and realised and then written. This world spoke to the early thinkers. Birds spoke to them, animals spoke to them, the sun and the moon spoke to them; and little by little they realised things, and got into the heart of nature. Not by cogitation not by the force of logic, not by picking the brains of others and making a big book, as is the fashion in modern times, not even as I do, by taking up one of their writings and making a long lecture, but by patient investigation and discovery they found out the truth. Its essential method was practice, and so it must be always. Religion is ever a practical science, and there never was nor will be any theological religion. It is practice first, and knowledge afterwards. The idea that souls come back is already there. Those persons who do good work with the idea of a result, get it, but the result is not permanent. There we get the idea of causation very beautifully put forward, that the effect is only commensurate with the cause. As the cause is, so the effect will be. The cause being finite, the effect must be finite. If the cause is eternal the effect can be eternal, but all these causes, doing good work, and all other things, are only finite causes, and as such cannot produce infinite result.

We now come to the other side of the question. As there cannot be an eternal heaven, on the same grounds, there cannot be an eternal hell. Suppose I am a very wicked man, doing evil every minute of my life. Still, my whole life here, compared with my eternal life, is nothing. If there be an eternal punishment, it will mean that there is an infinite effect produced by a finite cause, which cannot be. If I do good all my life, I cannot have an infinite heaven; it would be making the same mistake. But there is a third course which applies to those who have known the Truth, to those who have realised It. This is the only way to get beyond this veil of Mâyâ — to realise what Truth is; and the Upanishads indicate what is meant by realising the Truth.

It means recognising neither good nor bad, but knowing all as coming from the Self; Self is in everything. It means denying the universe; shutting your eyes to it; seeing the Lord in hell as well as in heaven; seeing the Lord in death as well as in life. This is the line of thought in the passage I have read to you; the earth is a symbol of the Lord, the sky is the Lord, the place we fill is the Lord, everything is Brahman. And this is to be seen, realised, not simply talked or thought about. We can see as its logical consequence that when the soul has realised that everything is full of the Lord, of Brahman, it will not care whether it goes to heaven, or hell, or anywhere else; whether it be born again on this earth or in heaven. These things have ceased to have any meaning to that soul, because every place is the same, every place is the temple of the Lord, every place has become holy and the presence of the Lord is all that it sees in heaven, or hell, or anywhere else. Neither good nor bad, neither life nor death — only the one infinite Brahman exists.

According to the Vedanta, when a man has arrived at that perception, he has become free, and he is the only man who is fit to live in this world. Others are not. The man who sees evil, how can he live in this world? His life is a mass of misery. The man who sees dangers, his life is a misery; the man who sees death, his life is a misery. That man alone can live in this world, he alone can say, "I enjoy this life, and I am happy in this life". who has seen the Truth, and the Truth in everything. By the by, I may tell you that the idea of hell does not occur in the Vedas anywhere. It comes with the Purânas much later. The worst punishment according to the Vedas is coming back to earth, having another chance in this world. From the very first we see the idea is taking the impersonal turn. The ideas of punishment and reward are very material, and they are only consonant with the idea of a human God, who loves one and hates another, just as we do. Punishment and reward are only admissible with the existence of such a God. They had such a God in the Samhita, and there we find the idea of fear entering, but as soon as we come to the Upanishads, the idea of fear vanishes, and the impersonal idea takes its place. It is naturally the hardest thing for man to understand, this impersonal idea, for he is always clinging on to the person. Even people who are thought to be great thinkers get disgusted at the idea of the Impersonal God. But to me it seems so absurd to think of God as an embodied man. Which is the higher idea, a living God, or a dead God? A God whom nobody sees, nobody knows, or a God Known?

The Impersonal God is a living God, a principle. The difference between personal and impersonal is this, that the personal is only a man, and the impersonal idea is that He is the angel, the man, the animal, and yet something more which we cannot see, because impersonality includes all personalities, is the sum total of everything in the universe, and infinitely more besides. "As the one fire coming into the world is manifesting itself in so many forms, and yet is infinitely more besides," so is the Impersonal.

We want to worship a living God. I have seen nothing but God all my life, nor have you. To see this chair you first see God, and then the chair in and through Him He is everywhere saying, "I am". The moment you feel "I am", you are conscious of Existence. Where shall we go to find God if we cannot see Him in our own hearts and in every living being? "Thou art the man, Thou art the woman, Thou art the girl, and Thou art the boy. Thou art the old man tottering with a stick. Thou art the young man walking in the pride of his strength." Thou art all that exists, a wonderful living God who is the only fact in the universe. This seems to many to be a terrible contradiction to the traditional God who lives behind a veil somewhere and whom nobody ever sees. The priests only give us an assurance that if we follow them, listen to their admonitions, and walk in the way they mark out for us — then when we die, they will give us a passport to enable us to see the face of God! What are all these heaven ideas but simply modifications of this nonsensical priestcraft?

Of course the impersonal idea is very destructive, it takes away all trade from the priests, churches, and temples. In India there is a famine now, but there are temples in each one of which there are jewels worth a king's ransom! If the priests taught this Impersonal idea to the people, their occupation would be gone. Yet we have to teach it unselfishly, without priestcraft. You are God and so am I; who obeys whom? Who worships whom? You are the highest temple of God; I would rather worship you than any temple, image, or Bible. Why are some people so contradictory in their thought? They are like fish slipping through our fingers. They say they are hard-headed practical men. Very good. But what is more practical than worshipping here, worshipping you? I see you, feel you, and I know you are God. The Mohammedan says, there is no God but Allah. The Vedanta says, there is nothing that is not God. It may frighten many of you, but you will understand it by degrees. The living God is within you, and yet you are building churches and temples and believing all sorts of imaginary nonsense. The only God to worship is the human soul in the human

body. Of course all animals are temples too, but man is the highest, the Taj Mahal of temples. If I cannot worship in that, no other temple will be of any advantage. The moment I have realised God sitting in the temple of every human body, the moment I stand in reverence before every human being and see God in him — that moment I am free from bondage, everything that binds vanishes, and I am free.

This is the most practical of all worship. It has nothing to do with theorising and speculation. Yet it frightens many. They say it is not right. They go on theorising about old ideals told them by their grandfathers, that a God somewhere in heaven had told some one that he was God. Since that time we have only theories. This is practicality according to them, and our ideas are impractical! No doubt, the Vedanta says that each one must have his own path, but the path is not the goal. The worship of a God in heaven and all these things are not bad, but they are only steps towards the Truth and not the Truth itself. They are good and beautiful, and some wonderful ideas are there, but the Vedanta says at every point, "My friend, Him whom you are worshipping as unknown, I worship as thee. He whom you are worshipping as unknown and are seeking for, throughout the universe, has been with you all the time. You are living through Him, and He is the Eternal Witness of the universe" "He whom all the Vedas worship, nay, more, He who is always present in the eternal 'I'. He existing, the whole universe exists. He is the light and life of the universe. If the 'I' were not in you, you would not see the sun, everything would be a dark mass. He shining, you see the world."

One question is generally asked, and it is this that this may lead to a tremendous amount of difficulty. Everyone of us will think, "I am God, and whatever I do or think must be good, for God can do no evil." In the first place, even taking this danger of misinterpretation for granted, can it be proved that on the other side the same danger does not exist? They have been worshipping a God in heaven separate from them, and of whom they are much afraid. They have been born shaking with fear, and all their life they will go on shaking. Has the world been made much better by this? Those who have understood and worshipped a Personal God, and those who have understood and worshipped an Impersonal God, on which side have been the great workers of the world — gigantic workers, gigantic moral powers? Certainly on the Impersonal. How can you expect morality to be developed through fear? It can never be. "Where one sees another, where one hears another, that is Maya. When one does not see another, when one does not hear another, when everything has become the Atman, who sees whom, who perceives whom?" It is all He, and all I, at the same time. The soul has become pure. Then, and then alone we understand what love is. Love cannot come through fear, its basis is freedom. When we really begin to love the world, then we understand what is meant by brotherhood or mankind, and not before.

So, it is not right to say that the Impersonal idea will lead to a tremendous amount of evil in the world, as if the other doctrine never lent itself to works of evil, as if it did not lead to sectarianism deluging the world with blood and causing men to tear each other to pieces. "My God is the greatest God, let us decide it by a free fight." That is the outcome of dualism all over the world. Come out into the broad open light of day, come out from the little narrow paths, for how can the infinite soul rest content to live and die in small ruts? Come out into the universe of Light. Everything in the universe is yours, stretch out your arms and embrace it with love. If you ever felt you wanted to do that, you have felt God.

You remember that passage in the sermon of Buddha, how he sent a thought of love towards the south, the north, the east, and the west, above and below, until the whole universe was filled with this lose, so grand, great, and infinite. When you have that feeling, you have true personality. The whole universe is one person; let go the little things. Give up the small for the Infinite, give up small enjoyments for infinite bliss. It is all yours, for the Impersonal includes the Personal. So God is Personal and Impersonal at the same time. And Man, the Infinite, Impersonal Man, is manifesting Himself as person. We the infinite have limited ourselves, as it were, into small parts. The Vedanta says that Infinity is our true nature; it will never vanish, it will abide for ever. But we are limiting ourselves by our Karma, which like a chain round our necks has dragged us into this limitation. Break that chain and be free. Trample law under your feet. There is no law in human nature, there is no destiny, no fate. How can there be law in infinity? Freedom is its watchword. Freedom is its nature, its birthright. Be free, and then have any number of personalities you like. Then we will play like the actor who comes upon the stage and plays the part of a beggar. Contrast him with the actual beggar walking in the streets. The scene is, perhaps, the same in both cases, the words are, perhaps, the same, but yet what difference! The one enjoys his beggary while the other is suffering misery from it. And what makes this difference? The one is free and the other is bound. The actor knows his beggary is not true, but that he has assumed it for play, while the real beggar thinks that it is his too familiar state and that he has to bear it whether he wills it or not. This is the law. So long as we have no knowledge of our real nature, we are beggars, jostled about by every force in nature; and made slaves of by everything in nature; we cry all over the world for help, but help never comes to us; we cry to imaginary beings, and yet it never comes. But still we hope help will come, and thus in weeping, wailing, and hoping, one life is passed, and the same play goes on and on.

Be free; hope for nothing from anyone. I am sure if you look back upon your lives you will find that you were always vainly trying to get help from others which never came. All the help that has come was from within yourselves. You only had the fruits of what you yourselves worked for, and yet you were strangely hoping all the time for help. A rich man's parlour is always full; but if you notice, you do not find the same people there. The visitors are always hoping that they will get something from those wealthy men, but they never do. So are our lives spent in hoping, hoping, hoping, which never comes to an end. Give up hope, says the Vedanta. Why should you hope? You have everything, nay, you are everything. What are you hoping for? If a king goes mad, and runs about trying to find the king of his country, he will never find him, because he is the king himself. He may go through every village and city in his own country, seeking in every house, weeping and wailing, but he will never find him, because he is the king himself. It is better that we know we are God and give up this fool's search after Him; and knowing that we are God we become happy and contented. Give up all these mad pursuits, and then play your part in the universe, as an actor on the stage.

The whole vision is changed, and instead of an eternal prison this world has become a playground; instead of

a land of competition it is a land of bliss, where there is perpetual spring, flowers bloom and butterflies flit about. This very world becomes heaven, which formerly was hell. To the eyes of the bound it is a tremendous place of torment, but to the eyes of the free it is quite otherwise. This one life is the universal life, heavens and all those places are here. All the gods are here, the prototypes of man. The gods did not create man after their type, but man created gods. And here are the prototypes, here is Indra, here is Varuna, and all the gods of the universe. We have been projecting our little doubles, and we are the originals of these gods, we are the real, the only gods to be worshipped. This is the view of the Vedanta, and this its practicality. When we have become free, we need not go mad and throw up society and rush off to die in the forest or the cave; we shall remain where we were, only we shall understand the whole thing. The same phenomena will remain, but with a new meaning. We do not know the world yet; it is only through freedom that we see what it is, and understand its nature. We shall see then that this so-called law, or fate, or destiny occupied only an infinitesimal part of our nature. It was only one side, but on the other side there was freedom all the time. We did not know this, and that is why we have been trying to save ourselves from evil by hiding our faces in the ground, like the hunted hare. Through delusion we have been trying to forget our nature, and yet we could not; it was always calling upon us, and all our search after God or gods, or external freedom, was a search after our real nature. We mistook the voice. We thought it was from the fire, or from a god or the sun, or moon, or stars, but at last we have found that it was from within ourselves. Within ourselves is this eternal voice speaking of eternal freedom; its music is eternally going on. Part of this music of the Soul has become the earth, the law, this universe, but it was always ours and always will be. In one word, the ideal of Vedanta is to know man as he really is, and this is its message, that if you cannot worship your brother man, the manifested God, how can you worship a God who is unmanifested?

Do you not remember what the Bible says, "If you cannot love your brother whom you have seen, how can you love God whom you have not seen?" If you cannot see God in the human face, how can you see him in the clouds, or in images made of dull, dead matter, or in mere fictitious stories of our brain? I shall call you religious from the day you begin to see God in men and women, and then you will understand what is meant by turning the left cheek to the man who strikes you on the right. When you see man as God, everything, even the tiger, will be welcome. Whatever comes to you is but the Lord, the Eternal, the Blessed One, appearing to us in various forms, as our father, and mother, and friend, and child — they are our own soul playing with us.

As our human relationships can thus be made divine, so our relationship with God may take any of these forms and we can look upon Him as our father, or mother, or friend, or beloved. Calling God Mother is a higher ideal than calling Him Father; and to call Him Friend is still higher; but the highest is to regard Him as the Beloved. The highest point of all is to see no difference between lover and beloved. You may remember, perhaps, the old Persian story, of how a lover came and knocked at the door of the beloved and was asked, "Who are you?" He answered, "It is I", and there was no response. A second time he came, and exclaimed, "I am here", but the door was not opened. The third time he came, and the voice asked from inside, "Who is there?" He replied, "I am thyself, my beloved", and the door opened. So is the relation between God and ourselves. He is in everything, He is everything. Every man and woman is the palpable, blissful, living God. Who says God is unknown? Who says He is to be searched after? We have found God eternally. We have been living in Him eternally; everywhere He is eternally known, eternally worshipped.

Then comes another idea, that other forms of worship are not errors. This is one of the great points to be remembered, that those who worship God through ceremonials and forms, however crude we may think them to be, are not in error. It is the journey from truth to truth, from lower truth to higher truth. Darkness is less light; evil is less good; impurity is less purity. It must always be borne in mind that we should see others with eyes of love, with sympathy, knowing that they are going along the same path that we have trodden. If you are free, you must know that all will be so sooner or later, and if you are free, how can you see the impermanent? If you are really pure, how do you see the impure? For what is within, is without. We cannot see impurity without having it inside ourselves. This is one of the practical sides of Vedanta, and I hope that we shall all try to carry it into our lives. Our whole life here is to carry this into practice, but the one great point we gain is that we shall work with satisfaction and contentment, instead of with discontent and dissatisfaction, for we know that Truth is within us, we have It as our birthright, and we have only to manifest It, and make It tangible.

Practical Vedanta: Part 3

(Delivered in London, 17th November 1896)

In the Chhâdogya Upanishad we read that a sage called Nârada came to another called Sanatkumâra, and asked him various questions, of which one was, if religion was the cause of things as they are. And Sanatkumara leads him, as it were, step by step, telling him that there is something higher than this earth, and something higher than that, and so on, till he comes to Âkâsha, ether. Ether is higher than light, because in the ether are the sun and the moon, lightning and the stars; in ether we live, and in ether we die. Then the question arises, if there is anything higher than that, and Sanatkumara tells him of Prâna. This Prana, according to the Vedanta, is the principle of life. It is like ether, an omnipresent principle; and all motion, either in the body or anywhere else, is the work of this Prana. It is greater than Akasha, and through it everything lives. Prana is in the mother, in the father, in the sister, in the teacher, Prana is the knower.

I will read another passage, where Shvetaketu asks his father about the Truth, and the father teaches him different things, and concludes by saying, "That which is the fine cause in all these things, of It are all these things made. That is the All, that is Truth, thou art That, O Shvetaketu." And then he gives various examples. "As a bee, O Shvetaketu, gathers honey from different flowers, and as the different honeys do not know that they are from various trees, and from various flowers, so all of us, having come to that Existence, know not that we have done so. Now, that which is that subtle essence, in It all that exists has its self. It is the True. It is the Self and thou, O Shvetaketu, are That." He gives another example of the rivers running down to the ocean. "As the rivers, when they are in the ocean, do not know that they have been various rivers, even so when we come out of that Existence, we do not know that we are That. O Shvetaketu, thou art That." So on he goes with his teachings.

Now there are two principles of knowledge. The one principle is that we know by referring the particular to the general, and the general to the universal; and the second is that anything of which the explanation is sought is to be explained so far as possible from its own nature. Taking up the first principle, we see that all our knowledge really consists of classifications, going higher and higher. When something happens singly, we are, as it were, dissatisfied. When it can be shown that the same thing happens again and again, we are satisfied and call it law. When we find that one apple falls, we are dissatisfied; but when we find that all apples fall, we call it the law of gravitation and are satisfied. The fact is that from the particular we deduce the general.

When we want to study religion, we should apply this scientific process. The same principle also holds good here, and as a fact we find that that has been the method all through. In reading these books from which I have been translating to you, the earliest idea that I can trace is this principle of going from the particular to the general. We see how the "bright ones" became merged into one principle; and likewise in the ideas of the cosmos we find the ancient thinkers going higher and higher — from the fine elements they go to finer and more embracing elements, and from these particulars they come to one omnipresent ether, and from that even they go to an all embracing force, or Prana; and through all this runs the principle, that one is not separate from the others. It is the very ether that exists in the higher form of Prana, or the higher form of Prana concretes, so to say, and becomes ether; and that ether becomes still grosser, and so on.

The generalization of the Personal God is another case in point. We have seen how this generalization was reached, and was called the sum total of all consciousness. But a difficulty arises — it is an incomplete generalization. We take up only one side of the facts of nature, the fact of consciousness, and upon that we generalise, but the other side is left out. So, in the first place it is a defective generalization. There is another insufficiency, and that relates to the second principle. Everything should be explained from its own nature. There may have been people who thought that every apple that fell to the ground was dragged down by a ghost, but the explanation is the law of gravitation; and although we know it is not a perfect explanation, yet it is much better than the other, because it is derived from the nature of the thing itself, while the other posits an extraneous cause. So throughout the whole range of our knowledge; the explanation which is based upon the nature of the thing itself is a scientific explanation, and an explanation which brings in an outside agent is unscientific.

So the explanation of a Personal God as the creator of the universe has to stand that test. If that God is outside of nature, having nothing to do with nature, and this nature is the outcome of the command of that God and produced from nothing, it is a very unscientific theory, and this has been the weak point of every Theistic religion throughout the ages. These two defects we find in what is generally called the theory of monotheism, the theory of a Personal God, with all the qualities of a human being multiplied very much, who, by His will, created this universe out of nothing and yet is separate from it. This leads us into two difficulties.

As we have seen, it is not a sufficient generalization, and secondly, it is not an explanation of nature from nature. It holds that the effect is not the cause, that the cause is entirely separate from the effect. Yet all human knowledge shows that the effect is but the cause in another form. To this idea the discoveries of modern science are tending every day, and the latest theory that has been accepted on all sides is the theory of evolution, the principle of which is that the effect is but the cause in another form, a readjustment of the cause, and the cause takes the form of the effect. The theory of creation out of nothing would be laughed at by modern scientists.

Now, can religion stand these tests? If there be any religious theories which can stand these two tests, they will be acceptable to the modern mind, to the thinking mind. Any other theory which we ask the modern man to believe, on the authority of priests, or churches, or books, he is unable to accept, and the result is a hideous mass of unbelief. Even in those in whom there is an external display of belief, in their hearts there is a tremendous amount of unbelief. The rest shrink away from religion, as it were, give it up, regarding it as priestcraft only.

Religion has been reduced to a sort of national form. It is one of our very best social remnants; let it remain. But the real necessity which the grandfather of the modern man felt for it is gone; he no longer finds it satisfactory to his reason. The idea of such a Personal God, and such a creation, the idea which is generally known as monotheism in every religion, cannot hold its own any longer. In India it could not hold its own because of the Buddhists, and that was the very point where they gained their victory in ancient times. They showed that if we allow that nature is possessed of infinite power, and that nature can work out all its wants, it is simply unnecessary to insist that there is something besides nature. Even the soul is unnecessary.

The discussion about substance and qualities is very old, and you will sometimes find that the old superstition lives even at the present day. Most of you have read how, during the Middle Ages, and, I am sorry to say, even much later, this was one of the subjects of discussion, whether qualities adhered to substance, whether length, breadth, and thickness adhered to the substance which we call dead matter, whether, the substance remaining, the qualities are there or not. To this our Buddhist says, "You have no ground for maintaining the existence of such a substance; the qualities are all that exist; you do not see beyond them." This is just the position of most of our modern agnostics. For it is this fight of the substance and qualities that, on a higher plane, takes the form of the fight between noumenon and phenomenon. There is the phenomenal world, the universe of continuous change, and there is something behind which does not change; and this duality of existence, noumenon and phenomenon, some hold, is true, and others with better reason claim that you have no right to admit the two, for what we see, feel, and think is only the phenomenon.

You have no right to assert there is anything beyond phenomenon; and there is no answer to this. The only answer we get is from the monistic theory of the Vedanta. It is true that only one exists, and that one is either phenomenon or noumenon. It is not true that there are two — something changing, and, in and through that, something which does not change; but it is the one and the same thing which appears as changing, and which is in reality unchangeable. We have come to think of the body, and mind, and soul as many, but really there is only one; and that one is appearing in all these various forms. Take the well-known illustration of the monists, the rope appearing as the snake. Some people, in the dark or through some other cause, mistake the rope for the snake, but when knowledge comes, the snake vanishes and it is found to be a rope. By this illustration we see that when the snake exists in the mind, the rope has vanished, and when the rope exists, the snake has gone. When we see phenomenon, and phenomenon only, around us, the noumenon has vanished, but when we see the noumenon, the unchangeable, it naturally follows that the phenomenon has vanished. Now, we understand better the position of both the realist and the idealist. The realist sees the phenomenon only, and the idealist looks to the noumenon. For the idealist, the really genuine idealist, who has truly arrived at the power of perception, whereby he can get away from all ideas of change, for him the changeful universe has vanished, and he has the right to say it is all delusion, there is no change. The realist at the same time looks at the changeful. For him the unchangeable has vanished, and he has a right to say this is all real.

What is the outcome of this philosophy? It is that the idea of Personal God is not sufficient. We have to get to something higher, to the Impersonal idea. It is the only logical step that we can take. Not that the personal idea would be destroyed by that, not that we supply proof that the Personal God does not exist, but we must go to the Impersonal for the explanation of the personal, for the Impersonal is a much higher generalization than the personal. The Impersonal only can be Infinite, the personal is limited. Thus we preserve the personal and do not destroy it. Often the doubt comes to us that if we arrive at the idea of the Impersonal God, the personal will be destroyed, if we arrive at the idea of the Impersonal man, the personal will be lost. But the Vedantic idea is not the destruction of the individual, but its real preservation. We cannot prove the individual by any other means but by referring to the universal, by proving that this individual is really the universal. If we think of the individual as separate from everything else in the universe, it cannot stand a minute. Such a thing never existed.

Secondly, by the application of the second principle, that the explanation of everything must come out of the nature of the thing, we are led to a still bolder idea, and one more difficult to understand. It is nothing less than this, that the Impersonal Being, our highest generalization, is in ourselves, and we are That. "O Shvetaketu, thou art That." You are that Impersonal Being; that God for whom you have been searching all over the universe is all the time yourself — yourself not in the personal sense but in the Impersonal. The man we know now, the manifested, is personalised, but the reality of this is the Impersonal. To understand the personal we have to refer it to the Impersonal, the particular must be referred to the general, and that Impersonal is the Truth, the Self of man.

There will be various questions in connection with this, and I shall try to answer them as we go on. Many difficulties will arise, but first let us clearly understand the position of monism. As manifested beings we appear to be separate, but our reality is one, and the less we think of ourselves as separate from that One, the better for us. The more we think of ourselves as separate from the Whole, the more miserable we become. From this monistic principle we get at the basis of ethics, and I venture to say that we cannot get any ethics from anywhere else. We know that the oldest idea of ethics was the will of some particular being or beings, but few are ready to accept that now, because it would be only a partial generalization. The Hindus say we must not do this or that because the Vedas say so, but the Christian is not going to obey the authority of the Vedas. The Christian says you must do this and not do that because the Bible says so. That will not be binding on those who do not believe in the Bible. But we must have a theory which is large enough to take in all these various grounds. Just as there are millions of people who are ready to believe in a Personal Creator, there have also been thousands of the brightest minds in this world who felt that such ideas were not sufficient for them, and wanted something higher, and wherever religion was not broad enough to include all these minds, the result was that the brightest minds in society were always outside of religion; and never was this so marked as at the present time, especially in Europe.

To include these minds, therefore, religion must become broad enough. Everything it claims must be judged from the standpoint of reason. Why religions should claim

that they are not bound to abide by the standpoint of reason, no one knows. If one does not take the standard of reason, there cannot be any true judgment, even in the case of religions. One religion may ordain something very hideous. For instance, the Mohammedan religion allows Mohammedans to kill all who are not of their religion. It is clearly stated in the Koran, "Kill the infidels if they do not become Mohammedans." They must be put to fire and sword. Now if we tell a Mohammedan that this is wrong, he will naturally ask, "How do you know that? How do you know it is not good? My book says it is." If you say your book is older, there will come the Buddhist, and say, my book is much older still. Then will come the Hindu, and say, my books are the oldest of all. Therefore referring to books will not do. Where is the standard by which you can compare? You will say, look at the Sermon on the Mount, and the Mohammedan will reply, look at the Ethics of the Koran. The Mohammedan will say, who is the arbiter as to which is the better of the two? Neither the New Testament nor the Koran can be the arbiter in a quarrel between them. There must be some independent authority, and that cannot be any book, but something which is universal; and what is more universal than reason? It has been said that reason is not strong enough; it does not always help us to get at the Truth; many times it makes mistakes, and, therefore, the conclusion is that we must believe in the authority of a church! That was said to me by a Roman Catholic, but I could not see the logic of it. On the other hand I should say, if reason be so weak, a body of priests would be weaker, and I am not going to accept their verdict, but I will abide by my reason, because with all its weakness there is some chance of my getting at truth through it; while, by the other means, there is no such hope at all.

We should, therefore, follow reason and also sympathise with those who do not come to any sort of belief, following reason. For it is better that mankind should become atheist by following reason than blindly believe in two hundred millions of gods on the authority of anybody. What we want is progress, development, realisation. No theories ever made men higher. No amount of books can help us to become purer. The only power is in realisation, and that lies in ourselves and comes from thinking. Let men think. A clod of earth never thinks; but it remains only a lump of earth. The glory of man is that he is a thinking being. It is the nature of man to think and therein he differs from animals. I believe in reason and follow reason having seen enough of the evils of authority, for I was born in a country where they have gone to the extreme of authority.

The Hindus believe that creation has come out of the Vedas. How do you know there is a cow? Because the word cow is in the Vedas. How do you know there is a man outside? Because the word man is there. If it had not been, there would have been no man outside. That is what they say. Authority with a vengeance! And it is not studied as I have studied it, but some of the most powerful minds have taken it up and spun out wonderful logical theories round it. They have reasoned it out, and there it stands — a whole system of philosophy; and thousands of the brightest intellects have been dedicated through thousands of years to the working out of this theory. Such has been the power of authority, and great are the dangers thereof. It stunts the growth of humanity, and we must not forget that we want growth. Even in all relative truth, more than the truth itself, we want the exercise. That is our life.

The monistic theory has this merit that it is the most rational of all the religious theories that we can conceive of. Every other theory, every conception of God which is partial and little and personal is not rational. And yet monism has this grandeur that it embraces all these partial conceptions of God as being necessary for many. Some people say that this personal explanation is irrational. But it is consoling; they want a consoling religion and we understand that it is necessary for them. The clear light of truth very few in this life can bear, much less live up to. It is necessary, therefore, that this comfortable religion should exist; it helps many souls to a better one. Small minds whose circumference is very limited and which require little things to build them up, never venture to soar high in thought. Their conceptions are very good and helpful to them, even if only of little gods and symbols. But you have to understand the Impersonal, for it is in and through that alone that these others can be explained. Take, for instance, the idea of a Personal God. A man who understands and believes in the Impersonal — John Stuart Mill, for example — may say that a Personal God is impossible, and cannot be proved. I admit with him that a Personal God cannot be demonstrated. But He is the highest reading of the Impersonal that can be reached by the human intellect, and what else is the universe but various readings of the Absolute? It is like a book before us, and each one has brought his intellect to read it, and each one has to read it for himself. There is something which is common in the intellect of all men; therefore certain things appear to be the same to the intellect of mankind. That you and I see a chair proves that there is something common to both our minds. Suppose a being comes with another sense, he will not see the chair at all; but all beings similarly constituted will see the same things. Thus this universe itself is the Absolute, the unchangeable, the noumenon;

and the phenomenon constitutes the reading thereof. For you will first find that all phenomena are finite. Every phenomenon that we can see, feel, or think of, is finite, limited by our knowledge, and the Personal God as we conceive of Him is in fact a phenomenon. The very idea of causation exists only in the phenomenal world, and God as the cause of this universe must naturally be thought of as limited, and yet He is the same Impersonal God. This very universe, as we have seen, is the same Impersonal Being read by our intellect. Whatever is reality in the universe is that Impersonal Being, and the forms and conceptions are given to it by our intellects. Whatever is real in this table is that Being, and the table form and all other forms are given by our intellects.

Now, motion, for instance, which is a necessary adjunct of the phenomenal, cannot be predicated of the Universal. Every little bit, every atom inside the universe, is in a constant state of change and motion, but the universe as a whole is unchangeable, because motion or change is a relative thing; we can only think of something in motion in comparison with something which is not moving. There must be two things in order to understand motion. The whole mass of the universe, taken as a unit, cannot move. In regard to what will it move? It cannot be said to change. With regard to what will it change? So the whole is the Absolute; but within it every particle is in a constant state of flux and change. It is unchangeable and changeable at the same time, Impersonal and Personal in one. This is our conception of the universe, of motion and of God, and that is what is meant by "Thou art That". Thus we see that the Impersonal instead of doing away with the personal, the Absolute instead of pulling down the relative, only explains it to the full satisfaction of our reason and heart. The Personal God and all that exists in the universe are the same Impersonal Being seen through our minds. When we shall be rid of our minds, our little personalities, we shall become one with It. This is what is meant by "Thou art That". For we must know our true nature, the Absolute.

The finite, manifested man forgets his source and thinks himself to be entirely separate. We, as personalised, differentiated beings, forget our reality, and the teaching of monism is not that we shall give up these differentiations, but we must learn to understand what they are. We are in reality that Infinite Being, and our personalities represent so many channels through which this Infinite Reality is manifesting Itself; and the whole mass of changes which we call evolution is brought about by the soul trying to manifest more and more of its infinite energy. We cannot stop anywhere on this side of the Infinite; our power, and blessedness, and wisdom, cannot but grow into the Infinite. Infinite power and existence and blessedness are ours, and we have not to acquire them; they are our own, and we have only to manifest them.

This is the central idea of monism, and one that is so hard to understand. From my childhood everyone around me taught weakness; I have been told ever since I was born that I was a weak thing. It is very difficult for me now to realise my own strength, but by analysis and reasoning I gain knowledge of my own strength, I realise it. All the knowledge that we have in this world, where did it come from? It was within us. What knowledge is outside? None. Knowledge was not in matter; it was in man all the time. Nobody ever created knowledge; man brings it from within. It is lying there. The whole of that big banyan tree which covers acres of ground, was in the little seed which was, perhaps, no bigger than one eighth of a mustard seed; all that mass of energy was there confined. The gigantic intellect, we know, lies coiled up in the protoplasmic cell, and why should not the infinite energy? We know that it is so. It may seem like a paradox, but is true. Each one of us has come out of one protoplasmic cell, and all the powers we possess were coiled up there. You cannot say they came from food; for if you heap up food mountains high, what power comes out of it? The energy was there, potentially no doubt, but still there. So is infinite power in the soul of man, whether he knows it or not. Its manifestation is only a question of being conscious of it. Slowly this infinite giant is, as it were, waking up, becoming conscious of his power, and arousing himself; and with his growing consciousness, more and more of his bonds are breaking, chains are bursting asunder, and the day is sure to come when, with the full consciousness of his infinite power and wisdom, the giant will rise to his feet and stand erect. Let us all help to hasten that glorious consummation.

Practical Vedanta: Part 4

(Delivered in London, 18th November 1896)

We have been dealing more with the universal so far. This morning I shall try to place before you the Vedantic ideas of the relation of the particular to the universal. As we have seen, in the dualistic form of Vedic doctrines, the earlier forms, there was a clearly defined particular and limited soul for every being. There have been a great many theories about this particular soul in each individual, but the main discussion was between the ancient Vedantists and the ancient Buddhists, the former believing in the individual soul as complete in itself, the latter denying in toto the existence of such an individual soul. As I told you the other day, it is pretty much the same discussion you have in Europe as to substance and quality, one set holding that behind the qualities there is something as substance, in which the qualities inhere; and the other denying the existence of such a substance as being unnecessary, for the qualities may live by themselves. The most ancient theory of the soul, of course, is based upon the argument of self-identity — "I am I" — that the I of yesterday is the I of today, and the I of today will be the I of tomorrow; that in spite of all the changes that are happening to the body, I yet believe that I am the same I. This seems to have been the central argument with those who believed in a limited, and yet perfectly complete, individual soul.

On the other hand, the ancient Buddhists denied the necessity of such an assumption. They brought forward the argument that all that we know, and all that we possibly can know, are simply these changes. The positing of an unchangeable and unchanging substance is simply superfluous, and even if there were any such unchangeable thing, we could never understand it, nor should we ever be able to cognise it in any sense of the word. The same discussion you will find at the present time going on in Europe between the religionists and the idealists on the one side, and the modern positivists and agnostics on the other; one set believing there is something which does not change (of whom the latest representative is your Herbert Spencer), that we catch a glimpse of something which is unchangeable. And the other is represented by the modern Comtists and modern Agnostics. Those of you who were interested a few years ago in the discussions between Herbert Spencer and Frederick Harrison might have noticed that it was the same old difficulty, the one party standing for a substance behind the changeful, and the other party denying the necessity for such an assumption. One party says we cannot conceive of changes without conceiving of something which does not change; the other party brings out the argument that this is superfluous; we can only conceive of something which is changing, and as to the unchanging, we can neither know, feel, nor sense it.

In India this great question did not find its solution in very ancient times, because we have seen that the assumption of a substance which is behind the qualities, and which is not the qualities, can never be substantiated; nay, even the argument from self-identity, from memory, — that I am the I of yesterday because I remember it, and therefore I have been a continuous something — cannot be substantiated. The other quibble that is generally put forward is a mere delusion of words. For instance, a man may take a long series of such sentences as "I do", "I go", "I dream", "I sleep", "I move", and here you will find it claimed that the doing, going, dreaming etc., have been changing, but what remained constant was that "I". As such they conclude that the "I" is something which is constant and an individual in itself, but all these changes belong to the body. This, though apparently very convincing and clear, is based upon the mere play on words. The "I" and the doing, going, and dreaming may be separate in black and white, but no one can separate them in his mind.

When I eat, I think of myself as eating — am identified with eating. When I run, I and the running are not two separate things. Thus the argument from personal identity does not seem to be very strong. The other argument from memory is also weak. If the identity of my being is represented by my memory, many things which I have forgotten are lost from that identity. And we know that people under certain conditions forget their whole past. In many cases of lunacy a man will think of himself as made of glass, or as being an animal. If the existence of that man depends on memory, he has become glass, which not being the case we cannot make the identity of the Self depend on such a flimsy substance as memory. Thus we see that the soul as a limited yet complete and continuing identity cannot be established as separate from the qualities. We cannot establish a narrowed-down, limited existence to which is attached a bunch of qualities.

On the other hand, the argument of the ancient Buddhists seems to be stronger — that we do not know, and cannot know, anything that is beyond the bunch of qualities. According to them, the soul consists of a bundle of qualities called sensations and feelings. A mass of such is what is called the soul, and this mass is continually changing.

The Advaitist theory of the soul reconciles both these positions. The position of the Advaitist is that it is true that we cannot think of the substance as separate from the qualities, we cannot think of change and not-change at the same time; it would be impossible. But the very thing which is the substance is the quality; substance and quality are not two things. It is the unchangeable that is appearing as the changeable. The unchangeable substance of the universe is not something separate from it. The noumenon is not something different from the phenomena, but it is the very noumenon which has become the phenomena. There is a soul which is unchanging, and what we call feelings and perceptions, nay, even the body, are the very soul, seen from another point of view. We have got into the habit of thinking that we have bodies and souls and so forth, but really speaking, there is only one.

When I think of myself as the body, I am only a body; it is meaningless to say I am something else. And when I think of myself as the soul, the body vanishes, and the perception of the body does not remain. None can get the perception of the Self without his perception of the body having vanished, none can get perception of the substance without his perception of the qualities having vanished.

The ancient illustration of Advaita, of the rope being taken for a snake, may elucidate the point a little more. When a man mistakes the rope for a snake, the rope has vanished, and when he takes it for a rope, the snake has vanished, and the rope only remains. The ideas of dual or treble existence come from reasoning on insufficient data, and we read them in books or hear about them, until we come under the delusion that we really have a dual perception of the soul and the body; but such a perception never really exists. The perception is either of the body or of the soul. It requires no arguments to prove it, you can verify it in your own minds.

Try to think of yourself as a soul, as a disembodied something. You will find it to be almost impossible, and those few who are able to do so will find that at the time when they realise themselves as a soul they have no idea of the body. You have heard of, or perhaps have seen, persons who on particular occasions had been in peculiar states of mind, brought about by deep meditation, self-hypnotism, hysteria, or drugs. From their experience you may gather that when they were perceiving the internal something, the external had vanished for them. This shows that whatever exists is one. That one is appearing in these various forms, and all these various forms give rise to the relation of cause and effect. The relation of cause and effect is one of evolution — the one becomes the other, and so on. Sometimes the cause vanishes, as it were, and in its place leaves the effect. If the soul is the cause of the body, the soul, as it were vanishes for the time being, and the body remains; and when the body vanishes, the soul remains. This theory fits the arguments of the Buddhists that were levelled against the assumption of the dualism of body and soul, by denying the duality, and showing that the substance and the qualities are one and the same thing appearing in various forms.

We have seen also that this idea of the unchangeable can be established only as regards the whole, but never as regards the part. The very idea of part comes from the idea of change or motion. Everything that is limited we can understand and know, because it is changeable; and the whole must be unchangeable, because there is no other thing besides it in relation to which change would be possible. Change is always in regard to something which does not change, or which changes relatively less.

According to Advaita, therefore, the idea of the soul as universal, unchangeable, and immortal can be demonstrated as far as possible. The difficulty would be as regards the particular. What shall we do with the old dualistic theories which have such a hold upon us, and which we have all to pass through — these beliefs in limited, little, individual souls?

We have seen that we are immortal with regard to the whole; but the difficulty is, we desire so much to be immortal as parts of the whole. We have seen that we are Infinite, and that that is our real individuality. But we want so much to make these little souls individual. What becomes of them when we find in our everyday experience that these little souls are individuals, with only this reservation that they are continuously growing individuals? They are the same, yet not the same. The I of yesterday is the I of today, and yet not so, it is changed somewhat. Now, by getting rid of the dualistic conception, that in the midst of all these changes there is something that does not change, and taking the most modern of conceptions, that of evolution, we find that the "I" is a continuously changing, expanding entity.

If it be true that man is the evolution of a mollusc, the mollusc individual is the same as the man, only it has to become expanded a great deal. From mollusc to man it has been a continuous expansion towards infinity. Therefore the limited soul can be styled an individual which is continuously expanding towards the Infinite Individual. Perfect individuality will only be reached when it has reached the Infinite, but on this side of the Infinite it is a continuously changing, growing personality. One of the remarkable features of the Advaitist system of Vedanta is to harmonise the preceding systems. In many cases it helped the philosophy very much; in some cases it hurt it. Our ancient philosophers knew what you call the theory of evolution; that growth is gradual, step by step, and the recognition of this led them to harmonise all the preceding systems. Thus not one of these preceding ideas was rejected. The fault of the Buddhistic faith was that it had neither the faculty nor the perception of this continual, expansive growth, and for this reason it never even made an attempt to harmonise itself with the preexisting steps towards the ideal. They were rejected as useless and harmful.

This tendency in religion is most harmful. A man gets a new and better idea, and then he looks back on those he has given up, and forthwith decides that they were mischievous and unnecessary. He never thinks that, however crude they may appear from his present point of view, they were very useful to him, that they were necessary for him to reach his present state, and that everyone of us has to grow in a similar fashion, living first on crude ideas, taking benefit from them, and then arriving at a higher standard. With the oldest theories, therefore, the Advaita is friendly. Dualism and all systems that had preceded it are accepted by the Advaita not in a patronising way, but with the conviction that they are true manifestations of the same truth, and that they all lead to the same conclusions as the Advaita has reached.

With blessing, and not with cursing, should be preserved all these various steps through which humanity has to pass. Therefore all these dualistic systems have never been rejected or thrown out, but have been kept intact in the Vedanta; and the dualistic conception of an individual soul, limited yet complete in itself, finds its place in the Vedanta.

According to dualism, man dies and goes to other worlds, and so forth; and these ideas are kept in the Vedanta in their entirety. For with the recognition of growth in the Advaitist system, these theories are given their proper place by admitting that they represent only a partial view of the Truth.

From the dualistic standpoint this universe can only be looked upon as a creation of matter or force, can only be looked upon as the play of a certain will, and that will again can only be looked upon as separate from the universe. Thus a man from such a standpoint has to see himself as composed of a dual nature, body and soul, and this soul, though limited, is individually complete in itself. Such a man's ideas of immortality and of the future life would necessarily accord with his idea of soul. These phases have been kept in the Vedanta, and it is, therefore, necessary for me to present to you a few of the popular ideas of dualism. According to this theory, we have a body, of course, and behind the body there is what they call a fine body. This fine body is also made of matter, only very fine. It is the receptacle of all our Karma, of all our actions and impressions, which are ready to spring up into visible forms. Every thought that we think, every deed that we do, after a certain time becomes fine, goes into seed form, so to speak, and lives in the fine body in a potential form, and after a time it emerges again and bears its results. These results condition the life of man. Thus he moulds his own life. Man is not bound by any other laws excepting those which he makes for himself. Our thoughts, our words and deeds are the threads of the net which we throw round ourselves, for good or for evil. Once we set in motion a certain power, we have to take the full consequences of it. This is the law of Karma. Behind the subtle body, lives Jiva or the individual soul of man. There are various discussions about the form and the size of this individual soul. According to some, it is very small like an atom; according to others, it is not so small as that; according to others, it is very big, and so on. This Jiva is a part of that universal substance, and it is also eternal; without beginning it is existing, and without end it will exist. It is passing through all these forms in order to manifest its real nature which is purity. Every action that retards this manifestation is called an evil action; so with thoughts. And every action and every thought that helps the Jiva to expand, to manifest its real nature, is good. One theory that is held in common in India by the crudest dualists as well as by the most advanced non-dualists is that all the possibilities and powers of the soul are within it, and do not come from any external source. They are in the soul in potential form, and the whole work of life is simply directed towards manifesting those potentialities.

They have also the theory of reincarnation which says that after the dissolution of this body, the Jiva will have another, and after that has been dissolved, it will again have another, and so on, either here or in some other worlds; but this world is given the preference, as it is considered the best of all worlds for our purpose. Other worlds are conceived of as worlds where there is very little misery, but for that very reason, they argue, there is less chance of thinking of higher things there. As this world contains some happiness and a good deal of misery, the Jiva some time or other gets awakened, as it were, and thinks of freeing itself. But just as very rich persons in this world have the least chance of thinking of higher things, so the Jiva in heaven has little chance of progress, for its condition is the same as that of a rich man, only more intensified; it has a very fine body which knows no disease, and is under no necessity of eating or drinking, and all its desires are fulfilled. The Jiva lives there, having enjoyment after enjoyment, and so forgets all about its real nature. Still there are some higher worlds, where in spite of all enjoyments, its further evolution is possible. Some dualists conceive of the goal as the highest heaven, where souls will live with God for ever. They will have beautiful bodies and will know neither disease nor death, nor any other evil, and all their desires will be fulfilled. From time to time some of them will come back to this earth and take another body to teach human beings the way to God; and the great teachers of the world have been such. They were already free, and were living with God in the highest sphere; but their love and sympathy for suffering humanity was so great that they came and incarnated again to teach mankind the way to heaven.

Of course we know that the Advaita holds that this cannot be the goal or the ideal; bodilessness must be the ideal. The ideal cannot be finite. Anything short of the Infinite cannot be the ideal, and there cannot be an infinite body. That would be impossible, as body comes from limitation. There cannot be infinite thought, because thought comes from limitation. We have to go beyond the body, and beyond thought too, says the Advaita. And we have also seen that, according to Advaita, this freedom is not to be attained, it is already ours. We only forget it and deny it. Perfection is not to be attained, it is already within us. Immortality and bliss are not to be acquired, we possess them already; they have been ours all the time.

If you dare declare that you are free, free you are this moment. If you say you are bound, bound you will remain. This is what Advaita boldly declares. I have told you the ideas of the dualists. You can take whichever you like.

The highest ideal of the Vedanta is very difficult to understand, and people are always quarrelling about it, and the greatest difficulty is that when they get hold of certain ideas, they deny and fight other ideas. Take up what suits you, and let others take up what they need. If you are desirous of clinging to this little individuality, to this limited manhood, remain in it, have all these desires, and be content and pleased with them. If your experience of manhood has been very good and nice, retain it as long as you like; and you can do so, for you are the makers of your own fortunes; none can compel you to give up your manhood. You will be men as long as you like; none can prevent you. If you want to be angels, you will be angels, that is the law. But there may be others who do not want to be angels even. What right have you to think that theirs is a horrible notion? You may be frightened to lose a hundred pounds, but there may be others who would not even wink if they lost all the money they had in the world. There have been such men and still there are. Why do you dare to judge them according to your standard? You cling on to your limitations, and these little worldly ideas may be your highest ideal. You are welcome to them. It will be to you as you wish. But there are others who have seen the truth and cannot rest in these limitations, who have done with these things and want to get beyond. The world with all its enjoyments is a mere mud-puddle for them. Why do you want to bind them down to your ideas? You must get rid of this tendency once for all. Accord a place to everyone.

I once read a story about some ships that were caught in a cyclone in the South Sea Islands, and there was a picture of it in the Illustrated London News . All of them were wrecked except one English vessel, which weathered the storm. The picture showed the men who were going to be drowned, standing on the decks and cheering the people who were sailing through the storm (H.M.S. Calliope and the American men-of-war at Samoa. — Ed). Be brave and generous like that. Do not drag others down to where you are. Another foolish notion is that if we lose our little individuality, there will be no morality, no hope for humanity. As if everybody had been dying for humanity all the time! God bless you! If in every country there were two hundred men and women really wanting to do good to humanity, the millennium would come in five days. We know how we are dying for humanity! These are all tall talks, and nothing else. The history of the world shows that those who never thought of their little individuality were the greatest benefactors of the human race, and that the more men and women think of themselves, the less are they able to do for others. One is unselfishness, and the other selfishness. Clinging on to little enjoyments, and to desire the continuation and repetition of this state of things is utter selfishness. It arises not from any desire for truth, its genesis is not in kindness for other beings, but in the utter selfishness of the human heart, in the idea, "I will have everything, and do not care for anyone else." This is as it appears to me. I would like to see more moral men in the world like some of those grand old prophets and sages of ancient times who would have given up a hundred lives if they could by so doing benefit one little animal! Talk of morality and doing good to others! Silly talk of the present time!

I would like to see moral men like Gautama Buddha, who did not believe in a Personal God or a personal soul, never asked about them, but was a perfect agnostic, and yet was ready to lay down his life for anyone, and worked all his life for the good of all, and thought only of the good of all. Well has it been said by his biographer, in describing his birth, that he was born for the good of the many, as a blessing to the many. He did not go to the forest to meditate for his own salvation; he felt that the world was burning, and that he must find a way out. "Why is there so much misery in the world ?" — was the one question that dominated his whole life. Do you think we are so moral as the Buddha?

The more selfish a man, the more immoral he is. And so also with the race. That race which is bound down to itself has been the most cruel and the most wicked in the whole world. There has not been a religion that has clung to this dualism more than that founded by the Prophet of Arabia, and there has not been a religion which has shed so much blood and been so cruel to other men. In the Koran there is the doctrine that a man who does not believe these teachings should be killed; it is a mercy to kill him! And the surest way to get to heaven, where there are beautiful houris and all sorts of sense-enjoyments, is by killing these unbelievers. Think of the bloodshed there has been in consequence of such beliefs!

In the religion of Christ there was little of crudeness; there is very little difference between the pure religion of Christ and that of the Vedanta. You find there the idea of oneness; but Christ also preached dualistic ideas to the people in order to give them something tangible to take hold of, to lead them up to the highest ideal. The same Prophet who preached, "Our Father which art in heaven", also preached, "I and my Father are one", and the same Prophet knew that through the "Father in heaven" lies the way to the "I and my Father are one". There was only blessing and love in the religion of Christ; but as soon as crudeness crept in, it was degraded into something not much better than the religion of the Prophet of Arabia. It was crudeness indeed — this fight for the little self, this clinging on to the "I", not only in this life, but also in the desire for its continuance even after death. This they declare to be unselfishness; this the foundation of morality! Lord help us, if this be the foundation of morality! And strangely enough, men and women who ought to know better think all morality will be destroyed if these little selves go and stand aghast at the idea that morality can only stand upon their destruction. The watchword of all well-being, of all moral good is not "I" but "thou". Who cares whether there is a heaven or a hell, who cares if there is a soul or not, who cares if there is an unchangeable or not? Here is the world, and it is full of misery. Go out into it as Buddha did, and struggle to lessen it or die in the attempt. Forget yourselves; this is the first lesson to be learnt, whether you are a theist or an atheist, whether you are an agnostic or a Vedantist, a Christian or a Mohammedan. The one lesson obvious to all is the destruction of the little self and the building up of the Real Self.

Two forces have been working side by side in parallel lines. The one says "I", the other says "not I". Their manifestation is not only in man but in animals, not only in animals but in the smallest worms. The tigress that plunges her fangs into the warm blood of a human being would give up her own life to protect her young. The most depraved man who thinks nothing of taking the lives of his brother men will, perhaps, sacrifice himself without any hesitation to save his starving wife and children. Thus throughout creation these two forces are working side by side; where you find the one, you find the other too. The one is selfishness, the other is unselfishness. The one is acquisition, the other is renunciation. The one takes, the other gives. From the lowest to the highest, the whole universe is the playground of these two forces. It does not require any demonstration; it is obvious to all.

What right has any section of the community to base the whole work and evolution of the universe upon one of these two factors alone, upon competition and struggle? What right has it to base the whole working of the universe upon passion and fight, upon competition and struggle? That these exist we do not deny; but what right has anyone to deny the working of the other force? Can any man deny that love, this "not I", this renunciation is the only positive power in the universe? That other is only the misguided employment of the power of love; the power of love brings competition, the real genesis of competition is in love. The real genesis of evil is in unselfishness. The creator of evil is good, and the end is also good. It is only misdirection of the power of good. A man who murders another is, perhaps, moved to do so by the love of his own child. His love has become limited to that one little baby, to the exclusion of the millions of other human beings in the universe. Yet, limited or unlimited, it is the same love.

Thus the motive power of the whole universe, in what ever way it manifests itself, is that one wonderful thing, unselfishness, renunciation, love, the real, the only living force in existence. Therefore the Vedantist insists upon that oneness. We insist upon this explanation because we cannot admit two causes of the universe. If we simply hold that by limitation the same beautiful, wonderful love appears to be evil or vile, we find the whole universe explained by the one force of love. If not, two causes of the universe have to be taken for granted, one good and the other evil, one love and the other hatred. Which is more logical? Certainly the one-force theory.

Let us now pass on to things which do not possibly belong to dualism. I cannot stay longer with the dualists. I am afraid. My idea is to show that the highest ideal of morality and unselfishness goes hand in hand with the highest metaphysical conception, and that you need not lower your conception to get ethics and morality, but, on the other hand, to reach a real basis of morality and ethics you must have the highest philosophical and scientific conceptions. Human knowledge is not antagonistic to human well-being. On the contrary, it is knowledge alone that will save us in every department of life — in knowledge is worship. The more we know the better for us. The Vedantist says, the cause of all that is apparently evil is the limitation of the unlimited. The love which gets limited into little channels and seems to be evil eventually comes out at the other end and manifests itself as God. The Vedanta also says that the cause of all this apparent evil is in ourselves. Do not blame any supernatural being, neither be hopeless and despondent, nor think we are in a place from which we can never escape unless someone comes and lends us a helping hand. That cannot be, says the Vedanta. We are like silkworms; we make the thread out of our own substance and spin the cocoon, and in course of time are imprisoned inside. But this is not for ever. In that cocoon we shall develop spiritual realisation, and like the butterfly come out free. This network of Karma we have woven around ourselves; and in our ignorance we feel as if we are bound, and weep and wail for help. But help does not come from without; it comes from within ourselves. Cry to all the gods in the universe. I cried for years, and in the end I found that I was helped. But help came from within. And I had to undo what I had done by mistake. That is the only way. I had to cut the net which I had thrown round myself, and the power to do this is within. Of this I am certain that not one aspiration, well-guided or ill-guided in my life, has been in vain, but that I am the resultant of all my past, both good and evil. I have committed many mistakes in my life; but mark you, I am sure of this that without every one of those mistakes I should not be what I am today, and so am quite satisfied to have made them. I do not mean that you are to go home and wilfully commit mistakes; do not misunderstand me in that way. But do not mope because of the mistakes you have committed, but know that in the end all will come out straight. It cannot be otherwise, because goodness is our nature, purity is our nature, and that nature can never be destroyed. Our essential nature always remains the same.

What we are to understand is this, that what we call mistakes or evil, we commit because we are weak, and we are weak because we are ignorant. I prefer to call them mistakes. The word sin, although originally a very good word, has got a certain flavour about it that frightens me. Who makes us ignorant? We ourselves. We put our hands over our eyes and weep that it is dark. Take the hands away and there is light; the light exists always for us, the self-effulgent nature of the human soul. Do you not hear what your modern scientific men say? What is the cause of evolution? Desire. The animal wants to do something, but does not find the environment favourable, and therefore develops a new body. Who develops it? The animal itself, its will. You have developed from the lowest amoeba. Continue to exercise your will and it will take you higher still. The will is almighty. If it is almighty, you may say, why cannot I do everything? But you are thinking only of your little self. Look back on yourselves from the state of the amoeba to the human being; who made all that? Your own will. Can you deny then that it is almighty? That which has made you come up so high can make you go higher still. What you want is character, strengthening of the will.

If I teach you, therefore, that your nature is evil, that you should go home and sit in sackcloth and ashes and weep your lives out because you took certain false steps, it will not help you, but will weaken you all the more, and I shall be showing you the road to more evil than good. If this room is full of darkness for thousands of years and you come in and begin to weep and wail, "Oh the darkness", will the darkness vanish? Strike a match and light comes in a moment. What good will it do you to think all your lives, "Oh, I have done evil, I have made many mistakes"? It requires no ghost to tell us that. Bring in the light and the evil goes in a moment. Build up your character, and manifest your real nature, the Effulgent, the Resplendent, the Ever-Pure, and call It up in everyone that you see. I wish that everyone of us had come to such a state that even in the vilest of human beings we could see the Real Self within, and instead of condemning them, say, "Rise thou effulgent one, rise thou who art always pure, rise thou birthless and deathless, rise almighty, and manifest thy true nature. These little manifestations do not befit thee." This is the highest prayer that the Advaita teaches. This is the one prayer, to remember our true nature, the God who is always within us, thinking of it always as infinite, almighty, ever-good, ever-beneficent, selfless, bereft of all limitations. And because that nature is selfless, it is strong and fearless; for only to selfishness comes fear. He who has nothing to desire for himself, whom does he fear, and what can frighten him? What fear has death for him? What fear has evil for him? So if we are Advaitists, we must think from this moment that our old self is dead and gone. The old Mr., Mrs., and Miss So-and-so are gone, they were mere superstitions, and what remains is the ever-pure, the ever-strong, the almighty, the all-knowing — that alone remains for us, and then all fear vanishes from us. Who can injure us, the omnipresent? All weakness has vanished from us, and our only work is to arouse this knowledge in our fellow beings. We see that they too are the same pure self, only they do not know it; we must teach them, we must help them to rouse up their infinite nature. This is what I feel to be absolutely necessary all over the world. These doctrines are old, older than many mountains possibly. All truth is eternal. Truth is nobody's property; no race, no individual can lay any exclusive claim to it. Truth is the nature of all souls. Who can lay an, special claim to it? But it has to be made practical, to be made simple (for the highest truths are always simple), so that it may penetrate every pore of human society, and become the property of the highest intellects and the commonest minds, of the man, woman, and child at the same time. All these ratiocinations of logic, all these bundles of metaphysics, all these theologies and ceremonies may have been good in their own time, but let us try to make things simpler and bring about the golden days when every man will be a worshipper, and the Reality in every man will be the object of worship.

The Way to the Realisation of a Universal Religion

(Delivered in the Universalist Church, Pasadena, California, 28th January 1900)

No search has been dearer to the human heart than that which brings to us light from God. No study has taken so much of human energy, whether in times past or present, as the study of the soul, of God, and of human destiny. However immersed we are in our daily occupations, in our ambitions, in our work, in the midst of the greatest of our struggles, sometimes there will come a pause; the mind stops and wants to know something beyond this world. Sometimes it catches glimpses of a realm beyond the senses, and a struggle to get at it is the result. Thus it has been throughout the ages, in all countries. Man has wanted to look beyond, wanted to expand himself; and all that we call progress, evolution, has been always measured by that one search, the search for human destiny, the search for God.

As our social struggles are represented amongst different nations by different social organizations, so is man's spiritual struggle represented by various religions; and as different social organizations are constantly quarrelling, are constantly at war with one another, so these spiritual organisations have been constantly at war with one another, constantly quarrelling. Men belonging to a particular social organisation claim that the right to live only belongs to them; and so long as they can, they want to exercise that right at the cost of the weak.

We know that just now there is a fierce struggle of that sort going on in South Africa. Similarly, each religious sect has claimed the exclusive right to live. And thus we find that though there is nothing that has brought to man more blessings than religion, yet at the same time, there is nothing that has brought more horror than religion. Nothing has made more for peace and love than religion; nothing has engendered fiercer hatred than religion. Nothing has made the brotherhood of man more tangible than religion; nothing has bred more bitter enmity between man and man than religion. Nothing has built more charitable institutions, more hospitals for men, and even for animals, than religion; nothing has deluged the world with more blood than religion. We know, at the same time, that there has always been an undercurrent of thought; there have been always parties of men, philosophers, students of comparative religion who have tried and are still trying to bring about harmony in the midst of all these jarring and discordant sects. As regards certain countries, these attempts have succeeded, but as regards the whole world, they have failed.

There are some religions which have come down to us from the remotest antiquity, which are imbued with the idea that all sects should be allowed to live, that every sect has a meaning, a great idea, imbedded within itself, and, therefore it is necessary for the good of the world and ought to be helped. In modern times the same idea is prevailing and attempts are made from time to time to reduce it to practice. These attempts do not always come up to our expectations, up to the required efficiency. Nay, to our great disappointment, we sometimes find that we are quarrelling all the more.

Now, leaving aside dogmatic study, and taking a common-sense view of the thing, we find at the start that there is a tremendous life-power in all the great religions of the world. Some may say that they are ignorant of this, but ignorance is no excuse. If a man says "I do not know what is going on in the external world, therefore things that are going on in the external world do not exist", that man is inexcusable. Now, those of you that watch the movement of religious thought all over the world are perfectly aware that not one of the great religions of the world has died; not only so, each one of them is progressive. Christians are multiplying, Mohammedans are multiplying, the Hindus are gaining ground, and the Jews also are increasing, and by their spreading all over the world and increasing rapidly, the fold of Judaism is constantly expanding.

Only one religion of the world — an ancient, great religion — has dwindled away, and that is the religion of Zoroastrianism, the religion of the ancient Persians. Under the Mohammedan conquest of Persia about a hundred thousand of these people came and took shelter in India and some remained in ancient Persia. Those that were in Persia, under the constant persecution of the Mohammedans, dwindled down till there are at most only ten thousand; in India there are about eighty thousand of them, but they do not increase. Of course, there is an initial difficulty; they do not convert others to their religion. And then, this handful of persons living in India, with the pernicious custom of cousin marriage, do not multiply. With this single exception, all the great religions are living, spreading, and increasing. We must remember that all the great religions of the world are very ancient, not one has been formed at the present time, and that every religion of the world owes its origin to the country between the Ganga and the Euphrates; not one great religion has arisen in Europe, not one in America, not one; every religion is of Asiatic origin and belongs to that part of the world. If what the modern scientists say is true, that the survival of the fittest is the test, these religions prove by their still living that they are yet fit for some people. There is a reason why they should live, they bring good to many. Look at the Mohammedans, how they are spreading in some places in Southern Asia, and spreading like fire in Africa. The Buddhists are spreading all over Central Asia, all the time. The Hindus, like the Jews, do not convert others; still gradually, other races are coming within Hinduism and adopting the manners and customs of the Hindus and falling into line with them. Christianity, you all know, is spreading — though I am not sure that the results are equal to the energy put forth. The Christians' attempt at propaganda has one tremendous defect — and that is the defect of all Western institutions: the machine consumes ninety per cent of the energy, there is too much machinery. Preaching has always been the business of the Asiatics. The Western people are grand in organisation, social institutions, armies, governments, etc.; but when it comes to preaching religion, they cannot come near the Asiatic, whose business it has been all the time, and he knows it, and he does not use too much machinery.

This then is a fact in the present history of the human race, that all these great religions exist and are spreading and multiplying. Now, there is a meaning, certainly, to this; and had it been the will of an All-wise and All-merciful Creator that one of these religions should exist and the rest should die, it would have become a fact long, long ago. If it were a fact that only one of these religions

is true and all the rest are false, by this time it would have covered the whole ground. But this is not so; not one has gained all the ground. All religions sometimes advance — sometimes decline. Now, just think of this: in your own country there are more than sixty millions of people, and only twenty-one millions professing religions of all sorts. So it is not always progress. In every country, probably, if the statistics are taken, you would find that religions are sometimes progressing and sometimes going back. Sects are multiplying all the time. If the claims of a religion that it has all the truth and God has given it all this truth in a certain book were true, why are there so many sects? Fifty years do not pass before there are twenty sects founded upon the same book. If God has put all the truth in certain books, He does not give us those books in order that we may quarrel over texts. That seems to be the fact. Why is it? Even if a book were given by God which contained all the truth about religion, it would not serve the purpose because nobody could understand the book. Take the Bible, for instance, and all the sects that exist amongst Christians; each one puts its own interpretation upon the same text, and each says that it alone understands that text and all the rest are wrong. So with every religion. There are many sects among the Mohammedans and among the Buddhists, and hundreds among the Hindus. Now, I bring these facts before you in order to show you that any attempt to bring all humanity to one method of thinking in spiritual things has been a failure and always will be a failure. Every man that starts a theory, even at the present day, finds that if he goes twenty miles away from his followers, they will make twenty sects. You see that happening all the time. You cannot make all conform to the same ideas: that is a fact, and I thank God that it is so. I am not against any sect. I am glad that sects exist, and I only wish they may go on multiplying more and more. Why? Simply because of this: If you and I and all who are present here were to think exactly the same thoughts, there would be no thoughts for us to think. We know that two or more forces must come into collision in order to produce motion. It is the clash of thought, the differentiation of thought, that awakes thought. Now, if we all thought alike, we would be like Egyptian mummies in a museum looking vacantly at one another's faces — no more than that! Whirls and eddies occur only in a rushing, living stream. There are no whirlpools in stagnant, dead water. When religions are dead, there will be no more sects; it will be the perfect peace and harmony of the grave. But so long as mankind thinks, there will be sects. Variation is the sign of life, and it must be there. I pray that they may multiply so that at last there will be as many sects as human beings, and each one will have his own method, his individual method of thought in religion.

But this thing exists already. Each one of us is thinking in his own way, but his natural course has been obstructed all the time and is still being obstructed. If the sword is not used directly, other means will be used. Just hear what one of the best preachers in New York says: he preaches that the Filipinos should be conquered because that is the only way to teach Christianity to them! They are already Catholics; but he wants to make them Presbyterians, and for this, he is ready to lay all this terrible sin of bloodshed upon his race. How terrible! And this man is one of the greatest preachers of this country, one of the best informed men. Think of the state of the world when a man like that is not ashamed to stand up and utter such arrant nonsense; and think of the state of the world when an audience cheers him! Is this civilisation? It is the old blood-thirstiness of the tiger, the cannibal, the savage, coming out once more under new names, new circumstances. What else can it be? If the state of things is such now, think of the horrors through which the world passed in olden times, when every sect was trying by every means in its power to tear to pieces the other sects. History shows that. The tiger in us is only asleep; it is not dead. When opportunities come, it jumps up and, as of old, uses its claws and fangs. Apart from the sword, apart from material weapons, there are weapons still more terrible — contempt, social hatred, and social ostracism. Now, these are the most terrible of all inflictions that are hurled against persons who do not think exactly in the same way as we do. And why should everybody think just as we do? I do not see any reason. If I am a rational man, I should be glad they do not think just as I do. I do not want to live in a grave-like land; I want to be a man in a world of men. Thinking beings must differ; difference is the first sign of thought. If I am a thoughtful man, certainly I ought to like to live amongst thoughtful persons where there are differences of opinion.

Then arises the question: How can all these varieties be true? If one thing is true, its negation is false. How can contradictory opinions be true at the same time? This is the question which I intend to answer. But I will first ask you: Are all the religions of the world really contradictory? I do not mean the external forms in which great thoughts are clad. I do not mean the different buildings, languages, rituals, books, etc. employed in various religions, but I mean the internal soul of every religion. Every religion has a soul behind it, and that soul may differ from the soul of another religion; but are they contradictory? Do they contradict or supplement each other? — that is the question. I took up the question when I was quite a boy, and have been studying it all my life. Thinking that my conclusion may be of some help to you, I place it before you. I believe that they are not contradictory; they are supplementary. Each religion, as it were, takes up one

part of the great universal truth, and spends its whole force in embodying and typifying that part of the great truth. It is, therefore, addition; not exclusion. That is the idea. System after system arises, each one embodying a great idea, and ideals must be added to ideals. And this is the march of humanity. Man never progresses from error to truth, but from truth to truth, from lesser truth to higher truth — but it is never from error to truth. The child may develop more than the father, but was the father inane? The child is the father plus something else. If your present state of knowledge is much greater than it was when you were a child, would you look down upon that stage now? Will you look back and call it inanity? Why, your present stage is the knowledge of the child plus something more.

Then, again, we also know that there may be almost contradictory points of view of the same thing, but they will all indicate the same thing. Suppose a man is journeying towards the sun, and as he advances he takes a photograph of the sun at every stage. When he comes back, he has many photographs of the sun, which he places before us. We see that not two are alike, and yet, who will deny that all these are photographs of the same sun, from different standpoints? Take four photographs of this church from different corners: how different they would look, and yet they would all represent this church. In the same way, we are all looking at truth from different standpoints, which vary according to our birth, education, surroundings, and so on. We are viewing truth, getting as much of it as these circumstances will permit, colouring the truth with our own heart, understanding it with our own intellect, and grasping it with our own mind. We can only know as much of truth as is related to us, as much of it as we are able to receive. This makes the difference between man and man, and occasions sometimes even contradictory ideas; yet we all belong to the same great universal truth.

My idea, therefore, is that all these religions are different forces in the economy of God, working for the good of mankind; and that not one can become dead, not one can be killed. Just as you cannot kill any force in nature, so you cannot kill any one of these spiritual forces. You have seen that each religion is living. From time to time it may retrograde or go forward. At one time, it may be shorn of a good many of its trappings; at another time it may be covered with all sorts of trappings; but all the same, the soul is ever there, it can never be lost. The ideal which every religion represents is never lost, and so every religion is intelligently on the march.

And that universal religion about which philosophers and others have dreamed in every country already exists. It is here. As the universal brotherhood of man is already existing, so also is universal religion. Which of you, that have travelled far and wide, have not found brothers and sisters in every nation? I have found them all over the world. Brotherhood already exists; only there are numbers of persons who fail to see this and only upset it by crying for new brotherhoods. Universal religion, too, is already existing. If the priests and other people that have taken upon themselves the task of preaching different religions simply cease preaching for a few moments, we shall see it is there. They are disturbing it all the time, because it is to their interest. You see that priests in every country are very conservative. Why is it so? There are very few priests who lead the people; most of them are led by the people and are their slaves and servants. If you say it is dry, they say it is so; if you say it is black, they say it is black. If the people advance, the priests must advance. They cannot lag behind. So, before blaming the priests — it is the fashion to blame the priest — you ought to blame yourselves. You only get what you deserve. What would be the fate of a priest who wants to give you new and advanced ideas and lead you forward? His children would probably starve, and he would be clad in rags. He is governed by the same worldly laws as you are. "If you go on," he says, "let us march." Of course, there are exceptional souls, not cowed down by public opinion. They see the truth and truth alone they value. Truth has got hold of them, has got possession of them, as it were, and they cannot but march ahead. They never look backward, and for them there are no people. God alone exists for them, He is the Light before them, and they are following that Light.

I met a Mormon gentleman in this country, who tried to persuade me to his faith. I said, "I have great respect for your opinions, but in certain points we do not agree — I belong to a monastic order, and you believe in marrying many wives. But why don't you go to India to preach?" Then he was astonished. He said, "Why, you don't believe in any marriage at all, and we believe in polygamy, and yet you ask me to go to your country!" I said, "Yes; my countrymen will hear every religious thought wherever it may come from. I wish you would go to India, first, because I am a great believer in sects. Secondly, there are many men in India who are not at all satisfied with any of the existing sects, and on account of this dissatisfaction, they will not have anything to do with religion, and, possibly, you might get some of them." The greater the number of sects, the more chance of people getting religion. In the hotel, where there are all sorts of food, everyone has a chance to get his appetite satisfied. So I want sects to multiply in every country, that more people may have a chance to be spiritual. Do not think that people do not like religion. I do not believe that. The preachers cannot give them what they need. The same man that may have been branded as an atheist, as a materialist, or what not, may meet a man who gives him the truth needed by him, and he may turn out the most spiritual man in the community. We can eat only in our own way. For instance, we Hindus eat with our fingers. Our fingers are suppler than yours, you cannot use your fingers the same way. Not only the food should be supplied, but it should be taken in your own particular way. Not only must you have the spiritual ideas, but they must come to you according to your own method. They must speak your own language, the language of your soul, and then alone they will satisfy you. When the man comes who speaks my language and gives truth in my language, I at once understand it and receive it for ever. This is a great fact.

Now from this we see that there are various grades and types of human minds and what a task religions take upon them! A man brings forth two or three doctrines and claims that his religion ought to satisfy all humanity. He goes out into the world, God's menagerie, with a little cage in hand, and says, "God and the elephant and everybody has to go into this. Even if we have to cut the elephant into pieces, he must go in." Again, there may be a sect with a few good ideas. Its followers say, "All men must come in! " "But there is no room for them." "Never mind! Cut them to pieces; get them in anyhow; if they don't get in, why, they will be damned." No preacher, no sect, have I ever met that pauses and asks, "Why is it that people do not listen to us?" Instead, they curse the people and say, "The people are wicked." They never ask, "How is it that people do not listen to my words? Why cannot I make them see the truth? Why cannot I speak in their language? Why cannot I open their eyes?" Surely, they ought to know better, and when they find people do not listen to them, if they curse anybody, it should be themselves. But it is always the people's fault! They never try to make their sect large enough to embrace every one.

Therefore we at once see why there has been so much narrow-mindedness, the part always claiming to be the whole; the little, finite unit always laying claim to the infinite. Think of little sects, born within a few hundred years out of fallible human brains, making this arrogant claim of knowledge of the whole of God's infinite truth! Think of the arrogance of it! If it shows anything, it is this, how vain human beings are. And it is no wonder that such claims have always failed, and, by the mercy of the Lord, are always destined to fail. In this line the Mohammedans were the best off; every step forward was made with the sword — the Koran in the one hand and the sword in the other: "Take the Koran, or you must die; there is no alternative! " You know from history how phenomenal was their success; for six hundred years nothing could resist them, and then there came a time when they had to cry halt. So will it be with other religions if they follow the same methods. We are such babes! We always forget human nature. When we begin life, we think that our fate will be something extraordinary, and nothing can make us disbelieve that. But when we grow old, we think differently. So with religions. In their early stages, when they spread a. little, they get the idea that they can change the minds of the whole human race in a few years, and go on killing and massacring to make converts by force; then they fail, and begin to understand

better. We see that these sects did not succeed in what they started out to do, which was a great blessing. Just think if one of those fanatical sects had succeeded all over the world, where would man be today? Now, the Lord be blessed that they did not succeed! Yet, each one represents a great truth; each religion represents a particular excellence — something which is its soul. There is an old story which comes to my mind: There were some ogresses who used to kill people and do all sorts of mischief; but they themselves could not be killed, until someone found out that their souls were in certain birds, and so long as the birds were safe nothing could destroy the ogresses. So, each one of us has, as it were, such a bird, where our soul is; has an ideal, a mission to perform in life. Every human being is an embodiment of such an ideal, such a mission. Whatever else you may lose, so long as that ideal is not lost, and that mission is not hurt, nothing can kill you. Wealth may come and go, misfortunes may pile mountains high, but if you have kept the ideal entire, nothing can kill you. You may have grown old, even a hundred years old, but if that mission is fresh and young in your heart, what can kill you? But when that ideal is lost and that mission is hurt, nothing can save you. All the wealth, all the power of the world will not save you. And what are nations but multiplied individuals? So, each nation has a mission of its own to perform in this harmony of races; and so long as that nation keeps to that ideal, that nation nothing can kill; but if that nation gives up its mission in life and goes after something else, its life becomes short, and it vanishes.

And so with religions. The fact that all these old religions are living today proves that they must have kept that mission intact; in spite of all their mistakes, in spite of all difficulties, in spite of all quarrels, in spite of all the incrustation of forms and figures, the heart of every one of them is sound — it is a throbbing, beating, living heart. They have not lost, any one of them, the great mission they came for. And it is splendid to study that mission. Take Mohammedanism, for instance. Christian people hate no religion in the world so much as Mohammedanism. They think it is the very worst form of religion that ever existed. As soon as a man becomes a Mohammedan, the whole of Islam receives him as a brother with open arms, without making any distinction, which no other religion does. If one of your American Indians becomes a Mohammedan, the Sultan of Turkey would have no objection to dine with him. If he has brains, no position is barred to him. In this country, I have never yet seen a church where the white man and the negro can kneel side by side to pray. Just think of that: Islam makes its followers all equal — so, that, you see, is the peculiar excellence of Mohammedanism. In many places in the Koran you find very sensual ideas of life. Never mind. What Mohammedanism comes to preach to the world is this practical brotherhood of all belonging to their faith. That is the essential part of the Mohammedan religion; and all the other ideas about heaven and of life etc.. are not Mohammedanism. They are accretions.

With the Hindus you will find one national idea — spirituality. In no other religion, in no other sacred books of the world, will you find so much energy spent in defining the idea of God. They tried to define the ideal of soul so that no earthly touch might mar it. The spirit must be divine; and spirit understood as spirit must not be made into a man. The same idea of unity, of the realisation of God, the omnipresent, is preached throughout. They think it is all nonsense to say that He lives in heaven, and all that. It is a mere human, anthropomorphic idea. All the heaven that ever existed is now and here. One moment in infinite time is quite as good as any other moment. If you believe in a God, you can see Him even now. We think religion begins when you have realised something. It is not believing in doctrines, nor giving intellectual assent, nor making declarations. If there is a God, have you seen Him? If you say "no", then what right have you to believe in Him? If you are in doubt whether there is a God, why do you not struggle to see Him? Why do you not renounce the world and spend the whole of your life for this one object? Renunciation and spirituality are the two great ideas of India, and it is because India clings to these ideas that all her mistakes count for so little.

With the Christians, the central idea that has been preached by them is the same: "Watch and pray, for the kingdom of Heaven is at hand" — which means, purify your minds and be ready! And that spirit never dies. You recollect that the Christians are, even in the darkest days, even in the most superstitious Christian countries, always trying to prepare themselves for the coming of the Lord, by trying to help others, building hospitals, and so on. So long as the Christians keep to that ideal, their religion lives.

Now an ideal presents itself to my mind. It may be only a dream. I do not know whether it will ever be realised in this world, but sometimes it is better to dream a dream, than die on hard facts. Great truths, even in a dream are good, better than bad facts. So, let us dream a dream.

You know that there are various grades of mind. You may be a matter-of-fact, common-sense rationalist: you do not care for forms and ceremonies; you want intellectual, hard, ringing facts, and they alone will satisfy you. Then there are the Puritans, the Mohammedans, who will not allow a picture or a statue in their place of worship. Very well! But there is another man who is more artistic. He wants a great deal of art — beauty of lines and curves, the colours, flowers, forms; he wants candles, lights, and all the insignia and paraphernalia of ritual, that he may see God. His mind takes God in those forms, as yours takes Him through the intellect. Then, there is the devotional man, whose soul is crying for God: he has no other idea but to worship God, and to praise Him. Then again, there is the philosopher, standing outside all these, mocking at them. He thinks, "What nonsense they are! What ideas about God!"

They may laugh at one another, but each one has a place in this world. All these various minds, all these various types are necessary. If there ever is going to be an ideal religion, it must be broad and large enough to supply food for all these minds. It must supply the strength of philosophy to the philosopher, the devotee's heart to the worshipper; to the ritualist, it will give all that the most marvellous symbolism can convey; to the poet, it will give as much of heart as he can take in, and other things besides. To make such a broad religion, we shall have to go back to the time when religions began and take them all in.

Our watchword, then, will be acceptance, and not exclusion. Not only toleration, for so-called toleration is often blasphemy, and I do not believe in it. I believe in acceptance. Why should I tolerate? Toleration means that I think that you are wrong and I am just allowing you to live. Is it not a blasphemy to think that you and I are allowing others to live? I accept all religions that were in the past, and worship with them all; I worship God with every one of them, in whatever form they worship Him. I shall go to the mosque of the Mohammedan; I shall enter the Christian's church and kneel before the crucifix; I shall enter the Buddhistic temple, where I shall take refuge in Buddha and in his Law. I shall go into the forest and sit down in meditation with the Hindu, who is trying to see the Light which enlightens the heart of every one.

Not only shall I do all these, but I shall keep my heart open for all that may come in the future. Is God's book finished? Or is it still a continuous revelation going on? It is a marvellous book — these spiritual revelations of the world. The Bible, the Vedas, the Koran, and all other sacred books are but so many pages, and an infinite number of pages remain yet to be unfolded. I would leave it open for all of them. We stand in the present, but open ourselves to the infinite future. We take in all that has been in the past, enjoy the light of the present, and open every window of the heart for all that will come in the future. Salutation to all the prophets of the past, to all the great ones of the present, and to all that are to come in the future!

The Open Secret

(Delivered at Los Angeles, Calif., 5th January 1900)

Whichever way we turn in trying to understand things in their reality, if we analyse far enough, we find that at last we come to a peculiar state of things, seemingly a contradiction: something which our reason cannot grasp and yet is a fact. We take up something — we know it is finite; but as soon as we begin to analyse it, it leads us beyond our reason, and we never find an end to all its qualities, its possibilities, its powers, its relations. It has become infinite. Take even a common flower, that is finite enough; but who is there that can say he knows all about the flower? There is no possibility of anyone's getting to the end of the knowledge about that one flower. The flower has become infinite — the flower which was finite to begin with. Take a grain of sand. Analyse it. We start with the assumption that it is finite, and at last we find that it is not, it is infinite; all the same, we have looked upon it as finite. The flower is similarly treated as a finite something.

So with all our thoughts and experiences, physical and mental. We begin, we may think, on a small scale, and grasp them as little things; but very soon they elude our knowledge and plunge into the abyss of the infinite. And the greatest and the first thing perceived is ourselves. We are also in the same dilemma about existence. We exist. We see we are finite beings. We live and die. Our horizon is narrow. We are here, limited, confronted by the universe all around. Nature can crush us out of existence in a moment. Our little bodies are just held together, ready to go to pieces at a moment's notice. We know that. In the region of action how powerless we are! Our will is being thwarted at every turn. So many things we want to do, and how few we can do! There is no limit to our willing. We can will everything, want everything, we can desire to go to the dogstar. But how few of our desires can be accomplished! The body will not allow it. Well, nature is against the accomplishment of our will. We are weak. What is true of the flower, of the grain of sand, of the physical world, and of every thought, is a hundredfold more true of ourselves. We are also in the same dilemma of existence, being finite and infinite at the same time. We are like waves in the ocean; the wave is the ocean and yet not the ocean. There is not any part of the wave of which you cannot say, "It is the ocean." The name "ocean" applies to the wave and equally to every other part of the ocean, and yet it is separate from the ocean. So in this infinite ocean of existence we are like wavelets. At the same time, when we want really to grasp ourselves, we cannot — we have become the infinite.

We seem to be walking in dreams. Dreams are all right in a dream-mind; but as soon as you want to grasp one of them, it is gone. Why? Not that it was false, but because it is beyond the power of reason, the power of the intellect to comprehend it. Everything in this life is so vast that the intellect is nothing in comparison with it. It refuses to be bound by the laws of the intellect! It laughs at the bondage the intellect wants to spread around it. And a thousandfold more so is this the case with the human soul. "We ourselves" — this is the greatest mystery of the universe.

How wonderful it all is! Look at the human eye. How easily it can be destroyed, and yet the biggest suns exist only because your eyes see them. The world exists because your eyes certify that it exists. Think of that mystery! These poor little eyes! A strong light, or a pin, can destroy them. Yet the most powerful engines of destruction, the most powerful cataclysms, the most wonderful of existences, millions of suns and stars and moons and earth — all depend for their existence upon, and have to be certified by, these two little things! They say, "Nature, you exist", and we believe nature exists. So with all our senses.

What is this? Where is weakness? Who is strong? What is great and what is small? What is high and what is low in this marvellous interdependence of existence where the smallest atom is necessary for the existence of the whole? Who is great and who is small? It is past finding out! And why? Because none is great and none is small. All things are interpenetrated by that infinite ocean; their reality is that infinite; and whatever there is on the surface is but that infinite. The tree is infinite; so is everything that you see or feel — every grain of sand, every thought, every soul, everything that exists, is infinite. Infinite is finite and finite infinite. This is our existence.

Now, that may be all true, but all this feeling after the Infinite is at present mostly unconscious. It is not that we have forgotten that infinite nature of ours: none can ever do that. Who can ever think that he can be annihilated? Who can think that he will die? None can. All our relation to the Infinite works in us unconsciously. In a manner, therefore, we forget our real being, and hence all this misery comes.

In practical daily life we are hurt by small things; we are enslaved by little beings. Misery comes because we think we are finite — we are little beings. And yet, how difficult it is to believe that we are infinite beings! In the midst of all this misery and trouble, when a little thing may throw me off my balance, it must be my care to believe that I am infinite. And the fact is that we are, and that consciously or unconsciously we are all searching after that something which is infinite; we are always seeking for something that is free.

There was never a human race which did not have a religion and worship some sort of God or gods. Whether the God or gods existed or not is no question; but what is the analysis of this psychological phenomenon? Why is all the world trying to find, or seeking for, a God? Why? Because in spite of all this bondage, in spite of nature and this tremendous energy of law grinding us down, never allowing us to turn to any side — wherever we go, whatever we want to do, we are thwarted by this law, which is everywhere — in spite of all this, the human soul never forgets its freedom and is ever seeking it. The search for freedom is the search of all religions; whether they know it or not, whether they can formulate it well or ill, the idea is there. Even the lowest man, the most ignorant, seeks for something which has power over nature's laws. He wants to see a demon, a ghost, a god — somebody who can subdue nature, for whom nature is not almighty, for whom there is no law. "Oh, for somebody who can break the law!" That is the cry coming from the human heart. We are always seeking for someone who breaks the law. The rushing engine speeds along the railway track; the little worm crawls out of its way. We at once say, "The engine is dead matter, a machine; and the worm is alive," because the worm attempted to break the law. The engine, with all its power and might, can never break the law. It is made to go in any direction man wants, and it cannot do otherwise; but the worm, small and little though it was, attempted to break the law and avoid the danger. It tried to assert itself against law, assert its freedom; and there was the sign of the future God in it.

Everywhere we see this assertion of freedom, this freedom of the soul. It is reflected in every religion in the shape of God or gods; but it is all external yet — for those who only see the gods outside. Man decided that he was nothing. He was afraid that he could never be free; so he went to seek for someone outside of nature who was free. Then he thought that there were many and many such free beings, and gradually he merged them all into one God of gods and Lord of lords. Even that did not satisfy him. He came a little closer to truth, a little nearer; and then gradually found that whatever he was, he was in some way connected with the God of gods and Lord of lords; that he, though he thought himself bound and low and weak, was somehow connected with that God of gods. Then visions came to him; thought arose and knowledge advanced. And he began to come nearer and nearer to that God, and at last found out that God and all the gods, this whole psychological phenomenon connected with the search for an all-powerful free soul, was but a reflection of his own idea of himself. And then at last he discovered that it was not only true that "God made man after His own image", but that it was also true that man made God after his own image. That brought out the idea of divine freedom. The Divine Being was always within, the nearest of the near. Him we had ever been seeking outside, and at last found that He is in the heart of our hearts. You may know the story of the man who mistook his own heartbeat for somebody knocking

at the door, and went to the door and opened it, but found nobody there, so he went back. Again he seemed to hear a knocking at the door, but nobody was there. Then he understood that it was his own heartbeat, and he had misinterpreted it as a knocking at the door. Similarly, man after his search finds out that this infinite freedom that he was placing in imagination all the time in the nature outside is the internal subject, the eternal Soul of souls; this Reality, he himself.

Thus at last he comes to recognise this marvellous duality of existence: the subject, infinite and finite in one — the Infinite Being is also the same finite soul. The Infinite is caught, as it were, in the meshes of the intellect and apparently manifests as finite beings, but the reality remains unchanged.

This is, therefore, true knowledge: that the Soul of our souls, the Reality that is within us, is That which is unchangeable, eternal, ever-blessed, ever-free. This is the only solid ground for us to stand upon.

This, then, is the end of all death, the advent of all immortality, the end of all misery. And he who sees that One among the many, that One unchangeable in the universe of change, he who sees Him as the Soul of his soul, unto him belongs eternal peace — unto none else.

And in the midst of the depths of misery and degradation, the Soul sends a ray of light, and man wakes up and finds that what is really his, he can never lose. No, we can never lose what is really ours. Who can lose his being? Who can lose his very existence? If I am good, it is the existence first, and then that becomes coloured with the quality of goodness. If I am evil, it is the existence first, and that becomes coloured with the quality of badness. That existence is first, last, and always; it is never lost, but ever present.

Therefore, there is hope for all. None can die; none can be degraded for ever. Life is but a playground, however gross the play may be. However we may receive blows, and however knocked about we may be, the Soul is there and is never injured. We are that Infinite.

Thus sang a Vedantin, "I never had fear nor doubt. Death never came to me. I never had father or mother: for I was never born. Where are my foes? — for I am All. I am the Existence and Knowledge and Bliss Absolute. I am It. I am It. Anger and lust and jealousy, evil thoughts and all these things, never came to me; for I am the Existence, the Knowledge, the Bliss Absolute. I am It. I am It."

That is the remedy for all disease, the nectar that cures death. Here we are in this world, and our nature rebels against it. But let us repeat, "I am It; I am It. I have no fear, nor doubt, nor death. I have no sex, nor creed, nor colour. What creed can I have? What sect is there to which I should belong? What sect can hold me? I am in every sect!"

However much the body rebels, however much the mind rebels, in the midst of the uttermost darkness, in the midst of agonising tortures, in the uttermost despair, repeat this, once, twice, thrice, ever more. Light comes gently, slowly, but surely it comes.

Many times I have been in the jaws of death, starving, footsore, and weary; for days and days I had had no food, and often could walk no farther; I would sink down under a tree, and life would seem ebbing away. I could not speak, I could scarcely think, but at last the mind reverted to the idea: "I have no fear nor death; I never hunger nor thirst. I am It! I am It! The whole of nature cannot crush me; it is my servant. Assert thy strength, thou Lord of lords and God of gods! Regain thy lost empire! Arise and walk and stop not!" And I would rise up, reinvigorated, and here am I, living, today. Thus, whenever darkness comes, assert the reality and everything adverse must vanish. For, after all, it is but a dream. Mountain-high though the difficulties appear, terrible and gloomy though all things seem, they are but Mâyâ. Fear not — it is banished. Crush it, and it vanishes. Stamp upon it, and it dies. Be not afraid. Think not how many times you fail. Never mind. Time is infinite. Go forward: assert yourself again and again, and light must come. You may pray to everyone that was ever born, but who will come to help you? And what of the way of death from which none knows escape? Help thyself out by thyself. None else can help thee, friend. For thou alone art thy greatest enemy, thou alone art thy greatest friend. Get hold of the Self, then. Stand up. Don't be afraid. In the midst of all miseries and all weakness, let the Self come out, faint and imperceptible though it be at first. You will gain courage, and at last like a lion you will roar out, "I am It! I am It!" "I am neither a man, nor a woman, nor a god, nor a demon; no, nor any of the animals, plants, or trees. I am neither poor nor rich, neither learned nor ignorant. All these things are very little compared with what I am: for I am It! I am It! Behold the sun and the moon and the stars: I am the light that is shining in them! I am the beauty of the fire! I am the power in the universe! For, I am It! I am It!

"Whoever thinks that I am little makes a mistake, for the Self is all that exists. The sun exists because I declare it does, the world exists because I declare it does. Without me they cannot remain, for I am Existence, Knowledge, and Bliss Absolute — ever happy, ever pure, ever beautiful. Behold, the sun is the cause of our vision, but is not itself ever affected by any defect in the eyes of any one; even so I am. I am working through all organs, working through everything, but never does the good and evil of work attach to me. For me there is no law, nor Karma. I own the laws of Karma. I ever was and ever am.

"My real pleasure was never in earthly things — in husband, wife, children, and other things. For I am like the infinite blue sky: clouds of many colours pass over it and play for a second; they move off, and there is the same unchangeable blue. Happiness and misery, good and evil, may envelop me for a moment, veiling the Self; but I am still there. They pass away because they are changeable. I shine, because I am unchangeable. If misery comes, I know it is finite, therefore it must die. If evil comes, I know it is finite, it must go. I alone am infinite and untouched by anything. For I am the Infinite, that Eternal, Changeless Self." — So sings one of our poets.

Let us drink of this cup, this cup that leads to everything that is immortal, everything that is unchangeable. Fear not. Believe not that we are evil, that we are finite,. that we can ever die. It is not true.

"This is to be heard of, then to be thought upon, and then to be meditated upon." When the hands work,. the mind should repeat, "I am It. I am It." Think of it, dream of it, until it becomes bone of your bones and; flesh of your flesh, until all the hideous dreams of littleness, of weakness, of misery, and of evil, have entirely vanished, and no more then can the Truth be hidden from you even for a moment.

The Way to Blessedness

I shall tell you a story from the Vedas tonight. The Vedas are the sacred scriptures of the Hindus and are a vast collection of literature, of which the last part is called the Vedanta, meaning the end of the Vedas. It deals with the theories contained in them, and more especially the philosophy with which we are concerned. It is written in archaic Sanskrit, and you must remember it was written thousands of years ago. There was a certain man who wanted to make a big sacrifice. In the religion of the Hindus, sacrifice plays a great part. There are various sorts of sacrifices. They make altars and pour oblations into the fire, and repeat various hymns and so forth; and at the end of the sacrifice they make a gift to the Brahmins and the poor. Each sacrifice has its peculiar gift. There was one sacrifice, where everything a man possessed had to be given up. Now this man, though rich, was miserly, and at the same time wanted to get a great name for having done this most difficult sacrifice. And when he did this sacrifice, instead of giving up everything he had, he gave away only his blind, lame, and old cows that would never more give milk. But he had a son called Nachiketas, a bright young boy, who, observing the poor gifts made by his father, and pondering on the demerit that was sure to accrue to him thereby, resolved to make amends for them by making a gift of himself. So he went to his father and said, "And to whom will you give me?" The father did not answer the boy, and the boy asked a second and a third time, when the father got vexed and said, "Thee I give unto Yama, thee I give unto Death." And the boy went straight to the kingdom of Yama. Yama was not at home, so he waited there. After three days Yama came and said to him, "O Brahmin, thou art my guest, and thou hast been here for three days without any food. I salute thee, and in order to repay thee for this trouble, I will grant thee three boons." Then the boy asked the first boon, "May my father's anger against me get calmed down," and the second boon was that he wanted to know about a certain sacrifice. And then came the third boon. "When a man dies, the question arises: What becomes of him: Some people say he ceases to exist. Others say that he exists. Please tell me what the answer is. This is the third boon that I want." Then Death answered, "The gods in ancient times tried to unravel the mystery; this mystery is so fine that it is hard to know. Ask for some other boon: do not ask this one. Ask for a long life of a hundred years. Ask for cattle and horses, ask for great kingdoms. Do not press me to answer this. Whatever man desires for his enjoyment, ask all that and I will fulfil it, but do not want to know this secret." "No sir," said the boy, ''man is not to be satisfied with wealth; if wealth were wanted, we should get it, if we have only seen you. We shall also live so long as you rule. What decaying mortal, living in the world below and possessed of knowledge, having gained the company of the undecaying and the immortal, will delight in long life, knowing the nature of the pleasure produced by song and sport? Therefore, tell me this secret about the great hereafter, I do not want anything else; that is what Nachiketas wants, the mystery of death." Then the God of death was pleased. We have been saying in the last two or three lectures that this Jnâna prepares the mind. So you see here that the first preparation is that a man must desire nothing else but the truth, and truth for truth's sake. See how this boy rejected all these gifts which Death offered him; possessions, property, wealth, long life, and everything he was ready to sacrifice for this one idea, knowledge only, the truth. Thus alone can truth come. The God of death became pleased. "Here are two ways," he said, "one of enjoyment, the other of blessedness. These two in various ways draw mankind. He becomes a sage who, of these two, takes up that which leads to blessedness, and he degenerates who takes up the road to enjoyment. I praise you, Nachiketas; you have not asked for desire. In various ways I tempted you towards the path of enjoyment; you resisted them all, you have known that knowledge is much higher than a life of enjoyment.

"You have understood that the man who lives in ignorance and enjoys, is not different from the brute beast. Yet there are many who, though steeped in ignorance, in the pride of their hearts, think that they are great sages and go round and round in many crooked ways, like the blind led by the blind. This truth, Nachiketas, never shines in the heart of those who are like ignorant children, deluded by a few lumps of earth. They do not understand this world, nor the other world. They deny this and the other one, and thus again and again come under my control. Many have not even the opportunity to hear about it; and many, though hearing, cannot know it, because the teacher must be wonderful; so must he be wonderful too unto whom the knowledge is carried. If the speaker is a man who is not highly advanced, then even a hundred times heard, and a hundred times taught, the truth never illumines the soul. Do not disturb your mind by vain arguments, Nachiketas; this truth only becomes effulgent in the heart which has been made pure. He who cannot be seen without the greatest difficulty, He who is hidden, He who has entered the cave of the heart of hearts — the Ancient One — cannot be seen with the external eyes; seeing Him with the eyes of the soul, one gives up both pleasure and pain. He who knows this secret gives up all his vain desires, and attains this superfine perception, and thus becomes ever blessed. Nachiketas, that is the way to blessedness. He is beyond all virtue, beyond all vice, beyond all duties, beyond all non-duties, beyond all existence, beyond all that is to be; he who knows this, alone knows. He whom all the Vedas seek, to see whom men undergo all sorts of asceticism, I will tell you His name: It is Om. This eternal Om is the Brahman, this is the immortal One; he who knows the secret of this — whatever he desires is his. This Self of man, Nachiketas, about which you seek to know, is never born, and never dies. Without beginning, ever existing, this Ancient One is not destroyed, when the body is destroyed. If the slayer thinks that he can slay, and if the slain man thinks he is slain, both are mistaken, for neither can the Self kill, nor can It be killed. Infinitely smaller than the smallest particle, infinitely greater than the greatest existence, the Lord of all lives in the cave of the heart of every being. He who has become sinless sees Him in all His glory, through the mercy of the same Lord. (We find that the mercy of God is one of the causes of God-realisation.) Sitting He goes far, lying He goes everywhere; who else but men of purified and subtle understanding are qualified to know the God in whom all conflicting attributes meet? Without body, yet living in the body, untouched, yet seemingly in contact, omnipresent — knowing the Âtman to be such, the sage gives up all misery. This Atman is not to be attained by the study of the Vedas, nor by the highest intellect, nor by much learning. Whom the Atman seeks, he gets the Atman; unto him He discloses His glory. He who is continuously doing evil deeds, he whose mind is not calm, he who cannot meditates he who is always disturbed and fickle — he cannot understand and realise this Atman who has entered the cave of the heart. This body, O Nachiketas, is the chariot, the organs of the senses are the horses, the mind is the reins, the intellect is the charioteer, and the soul is the rider in the chariot. When the soul joins himself with the charioteer, Buddhi or intellect, and then through it with the mind, the reins, and through it again with the organs, the horses, he is said to be the enjoyer; he perceives, he works, he acts. He whose mind is not under control, and who has no discrimination, his senses are not controllable like vicious horses in the hands of a driver. But he who has discrimination, whose mind is controlled, his organs are always controllable like good horses in the hands of a driver. He who has discrimination, whose mind is always in the way to understand truth, who is always pure — he receives that truth, attaining which there is no rebirth. This, O Nachiketas, is very difficult, the way is long, and it is hard to attain. It is only those who have attained the finest perception that can see it, that can understand it. Yet do not be frightened. Awake, be up and doing. Do not stop till you have reached the goal. For the sages say that the task is very difficult, like walking on the edge of a razor. He who is beyond the senses, beyond all touch, beyond all form, beyond all taste, the Unchangeable, the Infinite, beyond even intelligence, the Indestructible — knowing Him alone, we are safe from the jaws of death."

So far, we see that Yama describes the goal that is to be attained. The first idea that we get is that birth, death, misery, and the various tossings about to which we are subject in the world can only be overcome by knowing that which is real. What is real? That which never changes, the Self of man, the Self behind the universe. Then, again, it is said that it is very difficult to know Him. Knowing does not mean simply intellectual assent, it means realisation. Again and again we have read that

this Self is to be seen, to be perceived. We cannot see it with the eyes; the perception for it has to become superfine. It is gross perception by which the walls and books are perceived, but the perception to discern the truth has to be made very fine, and that is the whole secret of this knowledge. Then Yama says that one must be very pure. That is the way to making the perception superfine; and then he goes on to tell us other ways. That self-existent One is far removed from the organs. The organs or instruments see outwards, but the self-existing One, the Self, is seen inwards. You must remember the qualification that is required: the desire to know this Self by turning the eyes inwards. All these beautiful things that we see in nature are very good, but that is not the way to see God. We must learn how to turn the eyes inwards. The eagerness of the eyes to see outwards should be restricted. When you walk in a busy street, it is difficult to hear the man speak with whom you are walking, because of the noise of the passing carriages. He cannot hear you because there is so much noise. The mind is going outwards, and you cannot hear the man who is next to you. In the same way, this world around us is making such a noise that it draws the mind outwards. How can we see the Self? This going outwards must be stopped. That is what is meant by turning the eyes inwards, and then alone the glory of the Lord within will be seen.

What is this Self? We have seen that It is even beyond the intellect. We learn from the same Upanishad that this Self is eternal and omnipresent, that you and I and all of us are omnipresent beings, and that the Self is changeless. Now this omnipresent Being can be only one. There cannot be two beings who are equally omnipresent — how could that be? There cannot be two beings who are infinite, and the result is, there is really only one Self, and you, I, and the whole universe are but one, appearing as many. "As the one fire entering into the world manifests itself in various ways, even so that one Self, the Self of all, manifests Itself in every form." But the question is: If this Self is perfect and pure, and the One Being of the universe, what becomes of It when It goes into the impure body, the wicked body, the good body, and so on? How can It remain perfect? "The one sun is the cause of vision in every eye, yet it is not touched by the defects in the eyes of any." If a man has jaundice he sees everything as yellow; the cause of his vision is the sun, but his seeing everything as yellow does not touch the sun. Even so this One Being, though the Self of every one, is not touched by the purities or impurities outside. "In this world where everything is evanescent, he who knows Him who never changes, in this world of insentience, he who knows the one sentient Being, in this world of many, he who knows this One and sees Him in his own soul, unto him belongs eternal bliss, to none else, to none else. There the sun shines not, nor the stars, nor the lightning flashes, what to speak of fire? He shining, everything shines; through His light everything becomes effulgent. When all the desires that trouble the heart cease, then the mortal becomes immortal, and here one attains Brahman. When all the crookedness of the heart disappears, when all its knots are cut asunder, then alone the mortal becomes immortal. This is the way. May this study bless us; may it maintain us; may it give us strength, may it become energy in us; may we not hate each other; peace unto all!"

This is the line of thought that you will find in the Vedanta philosophy. We see first that here is a thought entirely different from what you see anywhere else in the world. In the oldest parts of the Vedas the search was the same as in other books, the search was outside. In some of the old, old books, the question was raised, "What was in the beginning? When there was neither aught nor naught, when darkness was covering darkness, who created all this?" So the search began. And they began to talk about the angels, the Devas, and all sorts of things, and later on we find that they gave it up as hopeless. In their day the search was outside and they could find nothing; but in later days, as we read in the Vedas, they had to look inside for the self-existent One. This Is the one fundamental idea in the Vedas, that our search in the stars, the nebulae, the Milky Way, in the whole of this external universe leads to nothing, never solves the problem of life and death. The wonderful mechanism inside had to be analysed, and it revealed to them the secret of the universe; nor star or sun could do it. Man had to be anatomised; not the body, but the soul of man. In that soul they found the answer. What was the answer they found? That behind the body, behind even the mind, there is the self-existent One. He dies not, nor is He born. The self-existent One it omnipresent, because He has no form. That which has no form or shape, that which is not limited by space or time, cannot live in a certain place. How can it? It is everywhere, omnipresent, equally present through all of us.

What is the soul of man? There was one party who held that there is a Being, God, and an infinite number of souls besides, who are eternally separate from God in essence, and form, and everything. This is dualism. This is the old, old crude idea. The answer given by another party was that the soul was a part of the infinite Divine Existence. Just as this body is a little world by itself, and behind it is the mind or thought, and behind that is the individual soul, similarly, the whole world is a body, and behind that is the universal mind, and behind that is the universal Soul. Just as this body is a portion of the universal body, so this mind is a portion of the universal mind, and the soul of man a portion of the universal Soul. This is what is called the Vishishtâdvaita, qualified monism. Now, we know that the universal Soul is infinite. How can infinity have parts? How can it be broken up, divided? It may be very poetic to say that I am a spark of the Infinite, but it is absurd to the thinking mind. What is meant by dividing Infinity? Is it something material that you can part or separate it into pieces? Infinite can never be divided. If that were possible, it would be no more Infinite. What is the conclusion then? The answer is, that Soul which is the universal is you; you are not a part but the whole of It. You are the whole of God. Then what are all these varieties? We find so many millions of individual souls. What are they? If the sun reflects upon millions of globules of water, in each globule is the form, the perfect image of the sun; but they are only images, and the real sun is only one. So this apparent soul that is in every one of us is only the image of God, nothing beyond that. The real Being who is behind, is that one God. We are all one there. As Self, there is only one in the universe. It is in me and you, and is only one; and that one Self has been reflected in all these various bodies as various different selves. But we do not know this; we think we are separate from each other and separate from Him. And so long as we think this, misery will be in the world. This is hallucination.

Then the other great source of misery is fear. Why does one man injure another? Because he fears he will not have enough enjoyment. One man fears that, perhaps, he will not have enough money, and that fear causes him to injure others and rob them. How can there be fear if there is only one existence? If a thunderbolt falls on my head, it was I who was the thunderbolt, because I am the only existence. If a plague comes, it is I; if a tiger comes, it is I. If death comes, it is I. I am both death and life. We see that fear comes with the idea that there are two in the universe. We have always heard it preached, "Love one another". What for? That doctrine was preached, but the explanation is here. Why should I love every one? Because they and I are one. Why should I love my brother? Because he and I are one. There is this oneness; this solidarity of the whole universe. From the lowest worm that crawls under our feet to the highest beings that ever lived — all have various bodies, but are the one Soul. Through all mouths, you eat; through all hands, you work; through all eyes, you see. You enjoy health in millions of bodies, you are suffering from disease in millions of bodies. When this idea comes, and we realise it, see it, feel it, then will misery cease, and fear with it. How can I die? There is nothing beyond me. Fear ceases, and then alone comes perfect happiness and perfect love. That universal sympathy, universal love, universal bliss, that never changes, raises man above everything. It has no reactions and no misery can touch it; but this little eating and drinking of the world always brings a reaction. The whole cause of it is this dualism, the idea that I am separate from the universe, separate from God. But as soon as we have realised that "I am He, I am the Self of the universe, I am eternally blessed, eternally free" — then will come real love, fear will vanish, and all misery cease.

Yajnavalkya and Maitreyi

We say, "That day is indeed a bad day on which you do not hear the name of the Lord, but a cloudy day is not a bad day at all." Yâjnavalkya was a great sage. You know, the Shastras in India enjoin that every man should give up the world when he becomes old. So Yajnavalkya said to his wife, "My beloved, here is all my money, and my possessions, and I am going away." She replied, "Sir, if I had this whole earth full of wealth, would that give me immortality?" Yajnavalkya said, "No, it will not. You will be rich, and that will be all, but wealth cannot give us immortality." She replied, "what shall I do to gain that through which I shall become immortal? If you know, tell me." Yajnavalkya replied, "You have been always my beloved; you are more beloved now by this question. Come, take your seat, and I will tell you; and when you have heard, meditate upon it." He said, "It is not for the sake of the husband that the wife loves the husband, but for the sake of the Âtman that she loves the husband, because she loves the Self. None loves the wife for the sake of the wife; but it is because one loves the Self that one loves the wife. None loves the children for the children; but because one loves the Self, therefore one loves the children. None loves wealth on account of the wealth; but because one loves the Self, therefore one loves wealth. None loves the Brâhmin for the sake of the Brahmin; but because one loves the Self, one loves the Brahmin. So, none loves the Kshatriya for the sake of the Kshatriya, but because one loves the Self. Neither does any one love the world on account of the world, but because one loves the Self. None, similarly, loves the gods on account of the gods, but because one loves the Self. None loves a thing for that thing's sake; but it is for the Self that one loves it. This Self, therefore, is to be heard, reasoned about, and meditated upon. O my Maitreyi, when that Self has been heard, when that Self has been seen, when that Self has been realised, then, all this becomes known." What do we get then? Before us we find a curious philosophy. The statement has been made that every love is selfishness in the lowest sense of the word: because I love myself, therefore I love another; it cannot be. There have been philosophers in modern times who have said that self is the only motive power in the world. That is true, and yet it is wrong. But this self is but the shadow of that real Self which is behind. It appears wrong and evil because it is small. That infinite love for the Self, which is the universe, appears to be evil, appears to be small, because it appears through a small part. Even when the wife loves the husband, whether she knows it or not, she loves the husband for that Self. It is selfishness as it is manifested in the world, but that selfishness is really but a small part of that Self-ness. Whenever one loves, one has to love in and through the Self. This Self has to be known. What is the difference? Those that love the Self without knowing what It is, their love is selfishness. Those that love, knowing what that Self is, their love is free; they are sages. "Him the Brahmin gives up who sees the Brahmin anywhere else but in the Self. Him the Kshatriya gives up who sees the Kshatriya anywhere else but in the Self. The world gives him up who sees this world anywhere but in that Atman. The gods give him up who loves the gods knowing them to be anywhere else but in the Atman. Everything goes away from him who knows everything as something else except the Atman. These Brahmins, these Kshatriyas, this world, these gods, whatever exists, everything is that Atman". Thus he explains what he means by love.

Every time we particularise an object, we differentiate it from the Self. I am trying to love a woman; as soon as that woman is particularised, she is separated from the Atman, and my love for her will not be eternal, but will end in grief. But as soon as I see that woman as the Atman, that love becomes perfect, and will never suffer. So with everything; as soon as you are attached to anything in the universe, detaching it from the universe as a whole, from the Atman, there comes a reaction. With everything that we love outside the Self, grief and misery will be the result. If we enjoy everything in the Self, and as the Self, no misery or reaction will come. This is perfect bliss. How to come to this ideal? Yajnavalkya goes on to tell us the process by which to reach that state. The universe is infinite: how can we take every particular thing and look at it as the Atman, without knowing the Atman? "As with a drum when we are at a distance we cannot catch the sound, we cannot conquer the sound; but as soon as we come to the drum and put our hand on it, the sound is conquered. When the conch-shell is being blown, we cannot catch or conquer the sound, until we come near and get hold of the shell, and then it is conquered. When the Vina is being played, when we have come to the Vina, we get to the centre whence the sound is proceeding. As when some one is burning damp fuel, smoke and sparks of various kinds come, even so, from this great One has been breathed out knowledge; everything has come out of Him. He breathed out, as it were, all knowledge. As to all water, the one goal is the ocean; as to all touch, the skin is the one centre; as of all smell, the nose is the one centre; as of all taste, the tongue is the one goal; as of all form, the eyes are the one goal; as of all sounds, the ears are the one goal; as of all thought, the mind is the one goal; as of all knowledge, the heart is the one goal; as of all work, the hands are the one goal; as a morsel of salt put into the sea-water melts away, and we cannot take it back, even so, Maitreyi, is this Universal Being eternally infinite; all knowledge is in Him. The whole universe rises from Him, and again goes down into Him. No more is there any knowledge, dying, or death." We get the idea that we have all come just like sparks from Him, and when you know Him, then you go back and become one with Him again. We are the Universal.

Maitreyi became frightened, just as everywhere people become frightened. Said she, "Sir, here is exactly where you have thrown a delusion over me. You have frightened me by saying there will be no more gods; all individuality will be lost. There will be no one to recognise, no one to love, no one to hate. What will become of us?" "Maitreyi, I do not mean to puzzle you, or rather let it rest here. You may be frightened. Where there are two, one sees another, one hears another, one welcomes another, one thinks of another, one knows another. But when the whole has become that Atman, who is seen by whom, who is to be heard by whom, who is to be welcomed by whom, who is to be known by whom?" That one idea was taken up by Schopenhauer and echoed in his philosophy. Through whom we know this universe, through what to know Him? How to know the knower? By what means can we know the knower? How can that be? Because in and through that we know everything. By what means can we know Him? By no means, for He is that means.

So far the idea is that it is all One Infinite Being. That is the real individuality, when there is no more division, and no more parts; these little ideas are very low, illusive. But yet in and through every spark of the individuality is shining that Infinite. Everything is a manifestation of the Atman. How to reach that? First you make the statement, just as Yajnavalkya himself tells us: "This Atman is first to be heard of." So he stated the case; then he argued it out, and the last demonstration was how to know That, through which all knowledge is possible. Then, last, it is to be meditated upon. He takes the contrast, the microcosm and the macrocosm, and shows how they are rolling on in particular lines, and how it is all beautiful. "This earth is so blissful, so helpful to every being; and all beings are so helpful to this earth: all these are manifestations of that Self-effulgent One, the Atman." All that is bliss, even in the lowest sense, is but the reflection of Him. All that is good is His reflection, and when that reflection is a shadow it is called evil. There are no two Gods. When He is less manifested, it is called darkness, evil; and when He is more manifested, it is called light. That is all. Good and evil are only a question of degree: more manifested or less manifested. Just take the example of our own lives. How many things we see in our childhood which we think to be good, but which really are evil, and how many things seem to be evil which are good! How the ideas change! How an idea goes up and up! What we thought very good at one time we do not think so good now. So good and evil are but superstitions, and do not exist. The difference is only in degree. It is all a manifestation of that Atman; He is being manifested in everything; only, when the manifestation is very thick we call it evil; and when it is very thin, we call it good. It is the best, when all covering goes away. So everything that is in the universe is to be meditated upon in that sense alone, that we can see it as all good, because it is the best. There is evil and there is good; and the apex, the centre, is the Reality. He is neither evil nor good; He is the best. The best can be only one, the good can be many and the evil many. There will be degrees of variation between the good and the evil, but the best is only one, and that best, when seen through thin coverings, we call different sorts of good, and when through thick covers, we call evil. Good and evil are different forms of superstition.

They have gone through all sorts of dualistic delusion and all sorts of ideas, and the words have sunk into the hearts of human beings, terrorising men and women and living there as terrible tyrants. They make us become tigers. All the hatred with which we hate others is caused by these foolish ideas which we have imbibed since our childhood — good and evil. Our judgment of humanity becomes entirely false; we make this beautiful earth a hell; but as soon as we can give up good and evil, it becomes a heaven.

"This earth is blissful ('sweet' is the literal translation) to all beings and all beings are sweet to this earth; they all help each other. And all the sweetness is the Atman, that effulgent, immortal One who is inside this earth." Whose is this sweetness? How can there be any sweetness but He? That one sweetness is manifesting itself in various ways. Wherever there is any love, any sweetness in any human being, either in a saint or a sinner, either in an angel or a murderer, either in the body, mind, or the senses, it is He. Physical enjoyments are but He, mental enjoyments are but He, spiritual enjoyments are but He. How can there be anything but He? How can there be twenty thousand gods and devils fighting with each other? Childish dreams! Whatever is the lowest physical enjoyment is He, and the highest spiritual enjoyment is He. There is no sweetness but He. Thus says Yajnavalkya. When you come to that state and look upon all things with the same eye, when you see even in the drunkard's pleasure in drink only that sweetness, then you have got the truth, and then alone you will know what happiness means, what peace means, what love means; and so long as toll make these vain distinctions, silly, childish, foolish superstitions, all sorts of misery will come. But that immortal One, the effulgent One, He is inside the earth, it is all His sweetness, and the same sweetness is in the body. This body is the earth, as it were, and inside all the powers of the body, all the enjoyments of the body, is He; the eyes see, the skin touches; what are all these enjoyments? That Self-effulgent One who is in the body, He is the Atman. This world, so sweet to all beings, and every being so sweet to it, is but the Self-effulgent; the Immortal is the bliss in that world. In us also, He is that bliss. He is the Brahman. "This air is so sweet to all beings, and all beings are so sweet to it. But He who is that Self-effulgent Immortal Being in the air — is also in this body. He is expressing Himself as the life of all beings. This sun is so sweet to all beings. All beings are so sweet to this sun. He who is the Self-effulgent Being in the sun, we reflect Him as the smaller light. What can be there but His reflection? He is in the body, and it is His reflection which makes us see the light. This moon is so sweet to all, and every one is so sweet to the moon, but that Self-effulgent and Immortal One who is the soul of that moon, He is in us expressing Himself as mind. This lightning is so beautiful, every one is so sweet to the lightning, but the Self-effulgent and Immortal One is the soul of this lightning, and is also in us, because all is that Brahman. The Atman, the Self, is the king of all beings." These ideas are very helpful to men; they are for meditation. For instance, meditate on the earth; think of the earth and at the same time know that we have That which is in the earth, that both are the same. Identify the body with the earth, and identify the soul with the Soul behind. Identify the air with the soul that is in the air and that is in me. They are all one, manifested in different forms. To realise this unity is the end and aim of all meditation, and this is what Yajnavalkya was trying to explain to Maitreyi.

0 SOUL, NATURE, AND GOD

According to the Vedanta philosophy, man consists of three substances, so to say. The outermost is the body, the gross form of man, in which are the instruments of sensation, such as the eyes, nose, ears, and so forth. This eye is not the organ of vision; it is only the instrument. Behind that is the organ. So, the ears are not the organs of hearing; they are the instruments, and behind them is the organ, or what, in modern physiology, is called the centre. The organs are called Indriyas in Sanskrit. If the centre which governs the eyes be destroyed, the eyes will not see; so with all our senses. The organs, again, cannot sense anything by themselves, until there be something else attached to them. That something is the mind. Many times you have observed that you were deeply engaged in a certain thought, and the clock struck and you did not hear it. Why? The ear was there; vibrations entered it and were carried into the brain, yet you did not hear, because the mind was not joined to the organ. The impressions of external objects are carried to the organs, and when the mind is attached to them, it takes the impressions and gives them, as it were, a colouring, which is called egoism, "I". Take the case of a mosquito biting me on the finger when I am engaged in some work. I do not feel it, because my mind is joined to something else. Later, when my mind is joined to the impression conveyed to the Indriyas, a reaction comes. With this reaction I become conscious of the mosquito. So even the mind joining itself to the organs is not sufficient; there must come the reaction in the form of will. This faculty from which the reaction comes, the faculty of knowledge

or intellect, is called "Buddhi" First, there must be the external instrument, next the organ, next the mind must join itself to the organ, then must come the reaction of intellect, and when all these things are complete, there immediately flashes the idea, "I and the external object", and there is a perception, a concept, knowledge. The external organ, which is only the instrument, is in the body, and behind that is the internal organ which is finer; then there is the mind, then the intellectual faculty, then egoism, which says, "I" — I see, I hear, and so forth. The whole process is carried on by certain forces; you may call them vital forces; in Sanskrit they are called Prâna. This gross part of man, this body, in which are the external instruments, is called in Sanskrit, Sthula Sharira, the gross body; behind it comes the series, beginning with the organs, the mind, the intellect, the egoism. These and the vital forces form a compound which is called the fine body, the Sukshma Sharira. These forces are composed of very fine elements, so fine that no amount of injury to this body can destroy them; they survive all the shocks given to this body. The gross body we see is composed of gross material, and as such it is always being renewed and changing continuously. But the internal organs, the mind, the intellect, and the egoism are composed of the finest material, so fine that they will endure for aeons and aeons. They are so fine that they cannot be resisted by anything; they can get through any obstruction. The gross body is non-intelligent, so is the fine, being composed of fine matter. Although one part is called mind, another the intellect, and the third egoism, yet we see at a glance that no one of them can be the "Knower". None of them can be the perceiver, the witness, the one for whom action is made, and who is the seer of the action. All these movements in the mind, or the faculty of intellection, or egoism, must be for some one else. These being composed of fine matter cannot be self-effulgent. Their luminosity cannot be in themselves. This manifestation of the table, for instance, cannot be due to any material thing. Therefore there must be some one behind them all, who is the real manifester, the real seer, the real enjoyer and He in Sanskrit is called the Atman, the Soul of man, the real Self of man. He it is who really sees things. The external instruments and the organs catch the impressions and convey them to the mind, and the mind to the intellect, and the intellect reflects them as on a mirror, and back of it is the Soul that looks on them and gives His orders and His directions. He is the ruler of all these instruments, the master in the house, the enthroned king in the body. The faculty of egoism, the faculty of intellection, the faculty of cogitation, the organs, the instruments, the body, all of them obey His commands. It is He who is manifesting all of these. This is the Atman of man. Similarly, we can see that what is in a small part of the universe must also be in the whole universe. If conformity is the law of the universe, every part of the universe must have been built on the same plan as the whole. So we naturally think that behind the gross material form which we call this universe of ours, there must be a universe of finer matter, which we call thought, and behind that there must be a Soul, which makes all this thought possible, which commands, which is the enthroned king of this universe. That soul which is behind each mind and each body is called Pratyagâtman, the individual Atman, and that Soul which is behind the universe as its guide, ruler, and governor, is God.

The next thing to consider is whence all these things come. The answer is: What is meant by coming? If it means that something can be produced out of nothing, it is impossible. All this creation, manifestation, cannot be produced out of zero. Nothing can be produced without a cause, and the effect is but the cause reproduced. Here is a glass. Suppose we break it to pieces, and pulverise it, and by means of chemicals almost annihilate it. Will it go back to zero? Certainly not. The form will break, but the particles of which it is made will be there; they will go beyond our senses, but they remain, and it is quite possible that out of these materials another glass may be made. If this is true in one case, it will be so in every case. Something cannot be made out of nothing. Nor can something be made to go back to nothing. It may become finer and finer, and then again grosser and grosser. The raindrop is drawn from the ocean in the form of vapour, and drifts away through the air to the mountains; there it changes again into water and flows back through hundreds of miles down to the mother ocean. The seed produces the tree. The tree dies, leaving only the seed. Again it comes up as another tree, which again ends in the seed, and so on. Look at a bird, how from; the egg it springs, becomes a beautiful bird, lives its life and then dies, leaving only other eggs, containing germs of future birds. So with the animals; so with men. Everything begins, as it were, from certain seeds, certain rudiments, certain fine forms, and becomes grosser and grosser as it develops; and then again it goes back to that fine form and subsides. The whole universe is going on in this way. There comes a time when this whole universe melts down and becomes finer and at last disappears entirely, as it were, but remains as superfine matter. We know through modern science and astronomy that this earth is cooling down, and in course of time it will become very cold, and then it will break to pieces and become finer and finer until it becomes ether once more. Yet the particles will all remain to form the material out of which another earth will be projected. Again that will disappear, and another will come out. So this universe will go back to its causes, and again its materials will come together and take form, like the wave that goes down, rises again, and takes shape. The acts of going back to causes and coming out again, taking form, are called in Sanskrit Sankocha and Vikâsha, which mean shrinking and expanding. The whole universe, as it were, shrinks, and then it expands again. To use the more accepted words of modern science, they are involved and evolved. You hear about evolution, how all forms grow from lower ones, slowly growing up and up. This is very true, but each evolution presupposes an involution. We know that the sum total of energy that is displayed in the universe is the same at all times, and that matter is indestructible. By no means can you take away one particle of matter. You cannot take away a foot-pound of energy or add one. The sum total is the same always. Only the manifestation varies, being involved and evolved. So this cycle is the evolution out of the involution of the previous cycle, and this cycle will again be involved, getting finer and finer, and out of that will come the next cycle. The whole universe is going on in this fashion. Thus we find that there is no creation in the sense that something is created out of nothing. To use a better word, there is manifestation, and God is the manifester of the universe. The universe, as it were, is being breathed out of Him, and again it shrinks into Him, and again He throws it out. A most beautiful simile is given in the Vedas — "That eternal One breathes out this universe and breathes it in." Just as we can breathe out a little particle of dust and breathe it in again. That is all very good, but the question may be asked: How we, it at the first cycle? The answer is: What is the meaning of a first cycle? There was none. If you can give a beginning to time, the whole concept of time will be destroyed. Try to think of a limit where time began, you have to think of time beyond that limit. Try to think where space begins, you will have to think of space beyond that. Time and

space are infinite, and therefore have neither beginning nor end. This is a better idea than that God created the universe in five minutes and then went to sleep, and since then has been sleeping. On the other hand, this idea will give us God as the Eternal Creator. Here is a series of waves rising and falling, and God is directing this eternal process. As the universe is without beginning and without end, so is God. We see that it must necessarily be so, because if we say there was a time when there was no creation, either in a gross or a fine form, then there was no God, because God is known to us as Sâkshi, the Witness of the universe. When the universe did not exist, neither did He. One concept follows the other. The idea of the cause we get from the idea of the effect, and if there is no effect, there will be no cause. It naturally follows that as the universe is eternal, God is eternal.

The soul must also be eternal. Why? In the first place we see that the soul is not matter. It is neither a gross body, nor a fine body, which we call mind or thought. It is neither a physical body, nor what in Christianity is called a spiritual body. It is the gross body and the spiritual body that are liable to change. The gross body is liable to change almost every minute and dies, but the spiritual body endures through long periods, until one becomes free, when it also falls away. When a man becomes free, the spiritual body disperses. The gross body disintegrates every time a man dies. The soul not being made of any particles must be indestructible. What do we mean by destruction? Destruction is disintegration of the materials out of which anything is composed. If this glass is broken into pieces, the materials will disintegrate, and that will be the destruction of the glass. Disintegration of particles is what we mean by destruction. It naturally follows that nothing that is not composed of particles can be destroyed, can ever be disintegrated. The soul is not composed of any materials. It is unity indivisible. Therefore it must be indestructible. For the same reasons it must also be without any beginning. So the soul is without any beginning and end.

We have three entities. Here is nature which is infinite, but changeful. The whole of nature is without beginning and end, but within it are multifarious changes. It is like a river that runs down to the sea for thousands of years. It is the same river always, but it is changing every minute, the particles of water are changing their position constantly. Then there is God, unchangeable, the ruler; and there is the soul unchangeable as God, eternal but under the ruler. One is the master, the other the servant, and the third one is nature.

God being the cause of the projection, the continuance, and the dissolution of the universe, the cause must be present to produce the effect. Not only so, the cause becomes the effect. Glass is produced out of certain materials and certain forces used by the manufacturer. In the glass there are those forces plus the materials. The forces used have become the force of adhesion, and if that force goes the glass will fall to pieces; the materials also are undoubtedly in the glass. Only their form is changed. The cause has become the effect. Wherever you see an effect you can always analyze it into a cause, the cause manifests itself as the effect. It follows, if God is the cause of the universe, and the universe is the effect, that God has become the universe. If souls are the effect, and God the cause, God has become the souls. Each soul, therefore, is a part of God. "As from a mass of fire an infinite number of sparks fly, even so from the Eternal One all this universe of souls has come out."

We have seen that there is the eternal God, and there is eternal nature. And there is also an infinite number of eternal souls. This is the first stage in religion, it is called dualism, the stage when man sees himself and God eternally separate, when God is a separate entity by Him, self and man is a separate entity by himself and nature is a separate entity by itself. This is dualism, which holds that the subject and the object are opposed to each other in everything. When man looks at nature, he is the subject and nature the object. He sees the dualism between subject and object. When he looks at God, he sees God as object and himself as the subject. They are entirely separate. This is the dualism between man and God. This is generally the first view of religion.

Then comes another view which I have just shown to you. Man begins to find out that if God is the cause of the universe and the universe the effect, God Himself must have become the universe and the souls, and he is but a particle of which God is the whole. We are but little beings, sparks of that mass of fire, and the whole universe is a manifestation of God Himself. This is the next step. In Sanskrit, it is called Vishishtâdvaita. Just as I have this body and this body covers the soul, and the soul is in and through this body, so this whole universe of infinite souls and nature forms, as it were, the body of God. When the period of involution comes, the universe becomes finer and finer, yet remains the body of God. When the gross manifestation comes, then also the universe remains the body of God. Just as the human soul is the soul of the human body and minds so God is the Soul of our souls. All of you have heard this expression in every religion, "Soul of our souls". That is what is meant by it. He, as it were, resides in them, guides them, is the ruler of them all. In the first view, that of dualism, each one of us is an individual, eternally separate from God and nature. In the second view, we are individuals, but not separate from God. We are like little particles floating in one mass, and that mass is God. We are individuals but one in God. We are all in Him. We are all parts of Him, and therefore we are One. And yet between man and man, man and God there is a strict individuality, separate and yet not separate.

Then comes a still finer question. The question is: Can infinity have parts? What is meant by parts of infinity? If you reason it out, you will find that it is impossible. Infinity cannot be divided, it always remains infinite. If it could be divided, each part would be infinite. And there cannot be two infinites. Suppose there were, one would limit the other, and both would be finite. Infinity can only be one, undivided. Thus the conclusion will be reached that the infinite is one and not many, and that one Infinite Soul is reflecting itself through thousands and thousands of mirrors, appearing as so many different souls. It is the same Infinite Soul, which is the background of the universe, that we call God. The same Infinite Soul also is the background of the human mind which we call the human soul.

COSMOLOGY

There are two worlds, the microcosm, and the macrocosm, the internal and the external. We get truth from both of these by means of experience. The truth gathered from internal experience is psychology, metaphysics, and religion; from external experience, the physical sciences. Now a perfect truth should be in harmony with experiences in both these worlds. The microcosm must bear testimony to the macrocosm, and the macrocosm to the microcosm; physical truth must have its counterpart in the internal world, and the internal world must have its verification outside. Yet, as a rule, we find that many of these truths are in conflict. At one period of the world's history, the internals become supreme, and they begin to fight the externals. At the present time the externals, the physicists, have become supreme, and they have put down many claims of psychologists and metaphysicians. So far as my knowledge goes, I find that the real, essential parts of psychology are in perfect accord with the essential parts of modern physical knowledge. It is not given to one individual to be great in every respect; it is not given to one race or nation to be equally strong in the research of all fields of knowledge. The modern European nations are very strong in their research of external physical knowledge, but they are not so strong in their study of the inner nature of man. On the other hand, the Orientals have not been very strong in their researches of the external physical world, but very strong in their researches of the internal. Therefore we find that Oriental physics and other sciences are not in accordance with Occidental Sciences; nor is Occidental psychology in harmony with Oriental psychology. The Oriental physicists have been routed by Occidental scientists. At the same time, each claims to rest on truth; and as we stated before, real truth in any field of knowledge will not contradict itself; the truths internal are in harmony with the truths external.

We all know the theories of the cosmos according to the modern astronomers and physicists; and at the same time we all know how woefully they undermine the theology of Europe, how these scientific discoveries that are made act as a bomb thrown at its stronghold; and we know how theologians have in all times attempted to put down these researches.

I want here to go over the psychological ideas of the Orientals about cosmology and all that pertains to it, and you will find how wonderfully they are in accordance with the latest discoveries of modern science; and where there is disharmony, you will find that it is modern science which lacks and not they. We all use the word nature. The old Sânkhya philosophers called it by two different names, Prakriti, which is very much the same as the word nature, and the more scientific name, Avyakta, undifferentiated, from which everything proceeds, such as atoms, molecules, and forces, mind, thought, and intelligence. It is startling to find that the philosophers and metaphysicians of India stated ages ago that mind is material. What are our present materialists trying to do, but to show that mind is as much a product of nature as the body? And so is thought, and, we shall find by and by, intelligence also: all issue from that nature which is called Avyakta, the undifferentiated. The Sankhyas define it as the equilibrium of three forces, one of which is called Sattva, another Rajas, and the third Tamas. Tamas, the lowest force, is that of attraction; a little higher is Rajas, that of repulsion; and the highest is the balance of these two, Sattva; so that when these two forces, attraction and repulsion, are held in perfect control by the Sattva there is no creation, no movement in the world. As soon as this equilibrium is lost, the balance is disturbed, and one of these forces gets stronger than the other, motion sets in, and creation begins. This state of things goes on cyclically, periodically. That is to say, there is a period of disturbance of the balance, when forces begin to combine and recombine, and things project outwards. At the same time, everything has a tendency to go back to the primal state of equilibrium, and the time comes when that total annihilation of all manifestation is reached. Again, after a period, the whole thing is disturbed, projected outwards, and again it slowly goes down — like waves. All motion, everything in this universe, can be likened to waves undergoing successive rise and fall. Some of these philosophers hold that the whole universe quiets down for a period. Others hold that this quieting down applies only to systems; that is to say, that while our system here, this solar system, will quiet down and go back into the undifferentiated state, millions of other systems will go the other way, and will project outwards. I should rather favour the second opinion, that this quieting down is not simultaneous over the whole of the universe, and that in different parts different things go on. But the principle remains the same, that all we see — that is, nature herself — is progressing in successive rises and falls. The one stage, falling down, going back to balance, the perfect equilibrium, is called Pralaya, the end of a cycle. The projection and the Pralaya of the universe have been compared by theistical writers in India to the outbreathing and inbreathing of God; God, as it were, breathes out the universe, and it comes into Him again. When it quiets down, what becomes of the universe? It exists, only in finer forms, in the form of cause, as it is called in the Sankhya philosophy. It does not get rid of causation, time, and space; they are there, only it comes to very fine and minute forms. Supposing that this whole universe begins to shrink, till every one of us becomes just a little molecule, we should not feel the change at all, because everything relating to us would be shrinking at the same time. The whole thing goes down, and again projects out, the cause brings out the effect, and so it goes on.

What we call matter in modern times was called by; the ancient psychologists Bhutas, the external elements. There is one element which, according to them, is eternal ; every other element is produced out of this one. It is called Âkâsha. It is somewhat similar to the idea of ether of the moderns, though not exactly similar. Along with this element, there is the primal energy called Prâna. Prana and Akasha combine and recombine and form the elements out of them. Then at the end of the Kalpa; everything subsides, and goes back to Akasha and Prana. There is in the Rig-Veda, the oldest human writing in existence, a beautiful passage describing creation, and it is most poetical — "When there was neither aught nor naught, when darkness was rolling over darkness, what existed?" and the answer is given, "It then existed without vibration". This Prana existed then, but there was no motion in it; Ânidavâtam means "existed without vibration". Vibration had stopped. Then when the Kalpa begins, after an immense interval, the Anidavatam (unvibrating atom) commences to vibrate, and blow after blow is given by Prana to Akasha. The atoms become condensed, and as they are condensed different elements are formed. We generally find these things very curiously translated; people do not go to the philosophers or the commentators for their translation,

and have not the brains to understand them themselves. A silly man reads three letters of Sanskrit and translates a whole book. They translate the, elements as air, fire, and so on; if they would go to the commentators, they would find they do not mean air or anything of the sort.

The Akasha, acted upon by the repeated blows of Prana, produces Vâyu or vibrations. This Vayu vibrates, and the vibrations growing more and more rapid result in friction giving rise to heat, Tejas. Then this heat ends in liquefaction, Âpah. Then that liquid becomes solid. We had ether, and motion, then came heat, then it became liquefied, and then it condensed into gross matter; and it goes back in exactly the reverse way. The solid will be liquefied and will then be converted into a mass of heat, and that will slowly get back into motion; that motion will stop, and this Kalpa will be destroyed. Then, again it will come back and again dissolve into ether. Prana cannot work alone without the help of Akasha. All that we know in the form of motion, vibration, or thought is a modification of the Prana, and everything that we know in the shape of matter, either as form or as resistance, is a modification of the Akasha. The Prana cannot live alone, or act without a medium; when it is pure Prana, it has the Akasha itself to live in, and when it changes into forces of nature, say gravitation, or centrifugal force, it must have matter. You have never seen force without matter or matter without force; what we call force and matter are simply the gross manifestations of these same things, which, when superfine, are called Prana and Akasha. Prana you can call in English life, the vital force; but you must not restrict it to the life of man; at the same time you must not identify it with Spirit, Atman. So this goes on. Creation cannot have either a beginning or an end; it is an eternal on-going.

We shall state another position of these old psychologists, which is that all gross things are the results of fine ones. Everything that is gross is composed of fine things, which they call the Tanmâtras, the fine particles. I smell a flower. To smell, something must come in contact with my nose; the flower is there, but I do not see it move towards me. That which comes from the flower and in contact with my nose is called the Tanmatra, fine molecules of that flower. So with heat, light and everything. These Tanmatras can again be subdivided into atoms. Different philosophers have different theories, and we know these are only theories. It is sufficient for our purpose to know that everything gross is composed of things that are very, very fine. We first get the gross elements which we feel externally, and then come the fine elements with which the nose, eyes, and ears come in contact. Ether waves touch my eyes; I cannot see them, yet I know they must come in contact with my eyes before I can see light.

Here are the eyes, but the eyes do not see. Take away the brain centre; the eyes will still be there, as also the picture of the outside world complete on the retinae; yet the eyes will not see. So the eyes are only a secondary instrument, not the organ of vision. The organ of vision is the nerve-centre in the brain. Likewise the nose is an instrument, and there is an organ behind it. The senses are simply the external instruments. It may be said that these different organs, Indriyas, as they are called in Sanskrit, are the real seats of perception.

It is necessary for the mind to be joined to an organ to perceive. It is a common experience that we do not hear the clock strike when we happen to be buried in study.

Why? The ear was there, the sound was carried through it to the brain; yet it was not heard, because the mind did not attach itself to the organ of hearing.

There is a different organ for each different instrument. For, if one served for all, we should find that when the mind joined itself to it, all the senses would be equally active. But it is not so, as we have seen from the instance of the clock. If there was only one organ for all the instruments, the mind would see and hear at the same time, would see and hear and smell at the same time, and it would be impossible for it not to do all these at one and the same time. Therefore it is necessary that there should be a separate organ for each sense. This has been borne out by modern physiology. It is certainly possible for us to hear and see at the same time, but that is because the mind attaches itself partially to the two centres.

What are the organs made of? We see that the instruments — eyes, nose, and ears — are made of gross materials. The organs are also made of matter. Just as the body is composed of gross materials, and manufactures Prana into different gross forces, so the organs are composed of the fine elements, Akasha, Vayu, Tejas, etc., and manufacture Prana into the finer forces of perception. The organs, the Prana functions, the mind and the Buddhi combined, are called the finer body of man — the Linga or Sukshma Sharira. The Linga Sharira has a real form because everything material must have a form.

The mind is called the Manas, the Chitta in Vritti or vibrating, the unsettled state. If you throw a stone in a lake, first there will be vibration, and then resistance. For a moment the water will vibrate and then it will react on the stone. So when any impression comes on the Chitta, it first vibrates a little. That is called the Manas. The mind carries the impression farther in, and presents it to the determinative faculty, Buddhi, which reacts. Behind Buddhi is Ahamkâra, egoism, the self-consciousness which says, "I am". Behind Ahamkara is Mahat, intelligence, the highest form of nature's existence. Each one is the effect of the succeeding one. In the case of the lake, every blow that comes to it is from the external world, while in the case of the mind, the blow may come either from the external or the internal world. Behind the intelligence is the Self of man, the Purusha, the Atman, the pure, the perfect, who alone is the seer, and for whom is all this change.

Man looks on all these changes; he himself is never impure; but through what the Vedantists call Adhyâsa, by reflection, by implication, he seems to be impure. It is like the appearance of a crystal when a red or a blue flower is brought before it: the colour is reflected on it, but the crystal itself is pure. We shall take it for granted that there are many selves, and each self is pure and perfect; various kinds of gross and fine matter superimpose themselves on the self and make it multicoloured. Why does nature do all this? Nature is undergoing all these changes for the development of the soul; all this creation is for the benefit of the soul, so that it may be free. This immense book which we call the universe is stretched out before man so that he may read; and he discovers eventually that he is an omniscient and omnipotent being. I must here tell you that some of our best psychologists do not believe in God in the sense in which you believe in Him. The father of our psychology, Kapila, denies the existence of God. His idea is that a Personal God is quite unnecessary; nature itself is sufficient to work out the whole of creation. What is called the Design Theory, he knocked on the head, and

said that a more childish theory was never advanced. But he admits a peculiar kind of God. He says we are all struggling to get free; and when we become free, we can, as it were, melt away into nature, only to come out at the beginning of the next cycle and be its ruler. We come out omniscient and omnipotent beings. In that sense we can be called Gods; you and I and the humblest beings can be Gods in different cycles. He says such a God will be temporal; but an eternal God, eternally omnipotent and ruler of the universe cannot be. If there was such a God, there would be this difficulty: He must be either a bound spirit or a free one. A God who is perfectly free would not create: there is no necessity for it. If He were bound, He would not create, because He could not: He would be powerless. In either case, there cannot be any omniscient or omnipotent eternal ruler. In our scriptures, wherever the word God is mentioned, he says, it means those human beings who have become free.

Kapila does not believe in the unity of all souls. His analysis, so far as it goes, is simply marvellous. He is the father of Indian thinkers; Buddhism and other systems are the outcome of his thought.

According to his psychology, all souls can regain their freedom and their natural rights, which are omnipotence and omniscience. But the question arises: Where is this bondage? Kapila says it is without beginning. But if it is without beginning, it must be without end, and we shall never be free. He says that though bondage is without beginning, it is not of that constant uniform character as the soul is. In other words, nature (the cause of bondage) is without beginning and end, but not in the same sense as soul, because nature has no individuality; it is like a river which gets a fresh body of water every moment; the sum total of these bodies of water is the river, but the river is not a constant quantity. Everything in nature is constantly changing, but the soul never changes; so, as nature is always changing, it is possible for the soul to come out of its bondage.

The whole of the universe is built upon the same plan as a part of it. So, just as I have a mind, there is a cosmic mind. As in the individual, so in the universal. There is the universal gross body; behind that, a universal fine body; behind that, a universal mind; behind that, a universal egoism, or consciousness; and behind that, a universal intelligence. And all this is in nature, the manifestation of nature, not outside of it.

We have the gross bodies from our parents, as also our consciousness. Strict heredity says my body is a part of my parents' bodies, the material of my consciousness and egoism is a part of my parents'. We can add to the little portion inherited from our parents by drawing upon the universal consciousness. There is an infinite store house of intelligence out of which we draw what we require; there is an infinite storehouse of mental force in the universe out of which we are drawing eternally; but the seed must come from the parents. Our theory is heredity coupled with reincarnation. By the law of heredity, the reincarnating soul receives from parents the material out of which to manufacture a man.

Some of the European philosophers have asserted that this world exists because I exist; and if I do not exist, the world will not exist. Sometimes it is stated thus: If all the people in the world were to die, and there were no more human beings, and no animals with powers of perception and intelligence, all these manifestations would disappear. But these European philosophers do not know the psychology of it, although they know the principle; modern philosophy has got only a glimpse of it. This becomes easy of understanding when looked at from the Sankhya point of view. According to Sankhya, it is impossible for anything to be, which has not as its material, some portion of my mind. I do not know this table as it is. An impression from it comes to the eyes, then to, the Indriya, and then to the mind; and the mind reacts, and that reaction is what I call the table. It is just the same as throwing a stone in a lake; the lake throws a wave towards the stone; this wave is what we know. What is external nobody knows; when I try to know it, it has to become that material which I furnish. I, with my own mind, have furnished the material for my eyes. There is something which is outside, which is only, the occasion, the suggestion, and upon that suggestion I project my mind; and it takes the form that I see. How do we all see the same things? Because we all have; similar parts of the cosmic mind. Those who have like minds will see like things, and those who have not will not see alike.

A STUDY OF THE SANKHYA PHILOSOPHY

Prakriti is called by the Sânkhya philosophers indiscrete, and defined as the perfect balance of the materials in it; and it naturally follows that in perfect balance there cannot be any motion. In the primal state before any manifestation, when there was no motion but perfect balance, this Prakriti was indestructible, because decomposition or death comes from instability or change. Again, according to the Sankhya, atoms are not the primal state. This universe does not come out of atoms: they may be the secondary or the tertiary state. The primordial material may form into atoms and become grosser and bigger things; and as far as modern investigations go, they rather point towards the same conclusion. For instance, in the modern theory of ether, if you say ether is atomic, it will not solve anything. To make it clearer, say that air is composed of atoms, and we know that ether is everywhere, interpenetrating, omnipresent, and that these air atoms are floating, as it were, in ether. If ether again be composed of atoms, there will still be spaces between every two atoms of ether. What fills up these? If you suppose that there is another ether still finer which does this, there will again be other spaces between the atoms of that finer ether which require filling up, and so it will be regressus ad infinitum , what the Sankhya philosophers call the "cause leading to nothing" So the atomic theory cannot be final. According to Sankhya, nature is omnipresent, one omnipresent mass of nature, in which are the causes of everything that exists. What is meant by cause? Cause is the fine state of the manifested state; the unmanifested state of that which becomes manifested. What do you mean by destruction? It is reverting to the cause If you have a piece of pottery and give it a blow, it is destroyed. What is meant by this is that the effects go back to their own nature, they materials out of which the pottery was created go back into their original state. Beyond this idea of destruction, any idea such as annihilation is on the face of it absurd. According to modern physical science, it can be demonstrated that all destruction means that which Kapila said ages ago — simply reverting to the cause. Going back to the finer form is all that is meant by destruction. You know how it can be demonstrated in a laboratory that matter is indestructible. At this present stage of our knowledge, if any man stands up and says that matter or this soul becomes annihilated, he is only making himself, ridiculous; it is only uneducated, silly people who would advance such a proposition; and it is curious that modern knowledge coincides with what those old philosophers taught. It must be so, and that is the proof of truth. They proceeded in their inquiry, taking up mind as the basis; they analysed the mental part of this universe and came to certain conclusions, which we, analysing the physical part, must come to, for they both must lead to the same centre.

You must remember that the first manifestation of this Prakriti in the cosmos is what the Sankhya calls "Mahat". We may call it intelligence — the great principle, its literal meaning. The first change in Prakriti is this intelligence; I would not translate it by self-consciousness, because that would be wrong. Consciousness is only a part of this intelligence. Mahat is universal. It covers all the grounds of sub-consciousness, consciousness, and super-consciousness; so any one state of consciousness, as applied to this Mahat, would not be sufficient. In nature, for instance, you note certain changes going on before your eyes which you see and understand, but there are other changes, so much finer, that no human perception can catch them. They are from the same cause, the same Mahat is making these changes. Out of Mahat comes universal egoism. These are all substance. There is no difference between matter and mind, except in degree. The substance is the same in finer or grosser form; one changes into the other, and this exactly coincides with the conclusions of modern physiological research. By believing in the teaching that the mind is not separate from the brain, you will be saved from much fighting and struggling. Egoism again changes into two varieties. In one variety it changes into the organs. Organs are of two kinds, organs of sensation and organs of reaction. They are not the eyes or the ears, but back of those are what you call brain-centres, and nerve-centres, and so on. This egoism, this matter or substance, becomes changed, and out of this material are manufactured these centres. Of the same substance is manufactured the other variety, the Tanmatras, fine particles of matter, which strike our organs of perception and bring about sensations. You cannot perceive them but only know they are there. Out of the Tanmatras is manufactured the gross matter — earth, water, and all the things that we see and feel. I want to impress this on your mind. It is very, hard to grasp it, because in Western countries the ideas are so queer about mind and matter. It is hard to get those impressions out of our brains. I myself had a tremendous difficulty, being educated in Western philosophy in my boyhood. These are all cosmic things. Think of this universal extension of matter, unbroken, one substance, undifferentiated, which is the first state of everything, and which begins to change in the same way as milk becomes curd. This first change is called Mahat. The substance Mahat changes into the grosser matter called egoism. The third change is manifested as universal sense-organs, and universal fine particles, and these last again combine and become this gross universe which with eyes, nose, and ears, we see, smell, and hear. This is the cosmic plan according to the Sankhya, and what is in the cosmos must also be microcosmic. Take an individual man. He has first a part of undifferentiated nature in him, and that material nature in him becomes changed into this Mahat, a small particle of this universal intelligence, and this particle of universal intelligence in him becomes changed into egoism, and then into the sense-organs and the fine particles of matter which combine and manufacture his body. I want this to be clear, because it is the stepping-stone to Sankhya, and it is absolutely necessary for you to understand it, because this is the basis of the philosophy of the whole world. There is no philosophy in the world that is not indebted to Kapila. Pythagoras came to India and studied this philosophy, and that was the beginning of the philosophy of the Greeks. Later, it formed the Alexandrian school, and still later, the Gnostic. It became divided into two; one part went to Europe and Alexandria, and the other remained in India; and out of this, the system of Vyasa was developed. The Sankhya philosophy of Kapila was the first rational system that the world ever saw. Every metaphysician in the world must pay homage to him. I want to impress on your mind that we are bound to listen to him as the great father of philosophy. This wonderful man, the most ancient of philosophers, is mentioned even in the Shruti: "O Lord, Thou who produced the sage Kapila in the Beginning." How wonderful his perceptions were, and if there is any proof required of the extraordinary power of the perception of Yogis, such men are the proof. They had no microscopes or telescopes. Yet how fine their perception was, how perfect and wonderful their analysis of things!

I will here point out the difference between Schopenhauer and the Indian philosophy. Schopenhauer says that desire, or will, is the cause of everything. It is the will to exist that make us manifest, but we deny this. The will is identical with the motor nerves. When I see an object there is no will; when its sensations are carried to the brain, there comes the reaction, which says "Do this", or "Do not do this", and this state of the ego-substance is what is called will. There cannot be a single particle of will which is not a reaction. So many things precede will. It is only a manufactured something out of the ego, and the ego is a manufacture of something still higher — the intelligence — and that again is a modification of the indiscrete nature. That was the Buddhistic idea, that whatever we see is the will. It is psychologically entirely wrong, because will can only be identified with the motor nerves. If you take out the motor nerves, a man has no will whatever. This fact, as is perhaps well known to you, has been found out after a long series of experiments made with the lower animals.

We will take up this question. It is very important to understand this question of Mahat in man, the great principle, the intelligence. This intelligence itself is modified into what we call egoism, and this intelligence is the cause of all the powers in the body. It covers the whole ground, sub-consciousness, consciousness, and super-consciousness. What are these three states? The sub-conscious state we find in animals, which we call instinct. This is almost infallible, but very limited. Instinct

rarely fails. An animal almost instinctively knows a poisonous herb from an edible one, but its instinct is very limited. As soon as something new comes, it is blind. It works like a machine. Then comes a higher state of knowledge which is fallible and makes mistakes often, but has a larger scope, although it is slow, and this you call reason. It is much larger than instinct, but instinct is surer than reason. There are more chances of mistakes in reasoning than in instinct. There is a still higher state of the mind, the super-conscious, which belongs only to Yogis, to men who have cultivated it. This is infallible and much more unlimited in its scope than reason. This is the highest state. So we must remember, this Mahat is the real cause of all that is here, that which manifests itself in various ways, covers the whole ground of sub-conscious, conscious, and super-conscious, the three states in which knowledge exists.

Now comes a delicate question which is being always asked. If a perfect God created the universe, why is there imperfection in it? What we call the universe is what we see, and that is only this little plane of consciousness and reason; beyond that we do not see at all. Now the very question is an impossible one. If I take only a small portion out of a mass of something and look at it, it seems to be inharmonious. Naturally. The universe is inharmonious because we make it so. How? What is reason? What is knowledge? Knowledge is finding the association about things. You go into the street and see a man and say, I know this is a man; because you remember the impressions on your mind, the marks on the Chitta. You have seen many men, and each one has made an impression on your mind; and as you see this man, you refer this to your store and see many similar pictures there; and when you see them, you are satisfied, and you put this new one with the rest. When a new impression comes and it has associations in your mind, you are satisfied; and this state of association is called knowledge. Knowledge is, therefore, pigeon-holing one experience with the already existing fund of experience, and this is one of the great proofs of the fact that you cannot have any knowledge until you have already a fund in existence. If you are without experience, as some European philosophers think, and that your mind is a tabula rasa to begin with, you cannot get any knowledge, because the very fact of knowledge is the recognition of the new by means of associations already existing in the mind. There must be a store at hand to which to refer a new impression. Suppose a child is born into this world without such a fund, it would be impossible for him ever to get any knowledge. Therefore, the child must have been previously in a state in which he had a fund, and so knowledge is eternally increasing. Slow me a way of getting round this argument. It is a mathematical fact. Some Western schools of philosophy also hold that there cannot be any knowledge without a fund of past knowledge. They have framed the idea that the child is born with knowledge. These Western philosophers say that the impressions with which the child comes into the world are not due to the child's past, but to the experiences of his forefathers: it is only hereditary transmission. Soon they will find out that this idea is all wrong; some German philosophers are now giving hard blows to these heredity ideas. Heredity is very good, but incomplete, it only explains the physical side. How do you explain the environments influencing us? Many causes produce one effect. Environment is one of the modifying effects. We make our own environment: as our past is, so we find the present environment. A drunken man naturally gravitates to the lowest slums of the city.

You understand what is meant by knowledge. Knowledge is pigeon-holing a new impression with old ones, recognising a new impression. What is meant by recognition? Finding associations with similar impressions that one already has. Nothing further is meant by knowledge. If that is the case, if knowledge means finding the associations, then it must be that to know anything we have to set the whole series of its similars. Is it not so? Suppose you take a pebble; to find the association, you have to see the whole series of pebbles similes to it. But with our perception of the universe as a whole we cannot do that, because in the pigeon-hole of our mind there is only one single record of the perception, we have no other perception of the same nature or class, we cannot compare it with any other. We cannot refer it to its associations. This bit of the universe, cut off by our consciousness, is a startling new thing, because we have not been able to find its associations. Therefore, we are struggling with it, and thinking it horrible, wicked, and bad; we may sometimes think it is good, but we always think it is imperfect. It is only when we find its associations that the universe can be known. We shall recognise it when we go beyond the universe and consciousness, and then the universe will stand explained. Until we can do that, all the knocking of our heads against a wall will never explain the universe, because knowledge is the finding of similars, and this conscious plane only gives us one single perception of it. So with our idea of God. All that we see of God is only a part just as we see only one portion of the universe, and all the rest is beyond human cognition. "I, the universal; so great am I that even this universe is but a part of Me." That is why we see God as imperfect, and do not understand Him. The only way to understand Him and the universe is to go beyond reason, beyond consciousness. "When thou goest beyond the heard and the hearing, the thought and the thinking, then alone wilt thou come to Truth." "Go thou beyond the scriptures, because they teach only up to nature, up to the three qualities." When we go beyond them, we find the harmony, and not before.

The microcosm and the macrocosm are built on exactly the same plan, and in the microcosm we know only one part, the middle part. We know neither the sub-conscious, nor the super-conscious. We know the conscious only. If a man stands up and says, "I am a sinner", he makes an untrue statement because he does not know himself. He is the most ignorant of men; of himself he knows only one part, because his knowledge covers only a part of the ground he is on. So with this universe, it is possible to know only a part of it with the reason, not the whole of it; for the sub-conscious, the conscious and the super-conscious, the individual Mahat and the universal Mahat, and all the subsequent modifications, constitute the universe.

What makes nature (Prakriti) change? We see so far that everything, all Prakriti, is Jada, insentient. It is all compound and insentient. Wherever there is law, it is proof that the region of its play is insentient. Mind, intelligence, will, and everything else is insentient. But they are all reflecting the sentiency, the "Chit" of some being who is beyond all this, whom the Sankhya philosophers call "Purusha". The Purusha is the unwitting cause of all the changes in the universe. That is to say, this Purusha, taking Him in the universal sense, is the God of the universe. It is said that the will of the Lord created the universe. It is very good as a common expression, but we see it cannot be true. How could it be will? Will is the third or fourth manifestation in nature. Many things exist before it, and what created them ? Will is a compound, and everything that is a compound is a product of nature. Will, therefore, could not create nature. So, to say that the will of the Lord created the universe is meaningless. Our will only covers a little portion of self-consciousness and moves our brain. It is not will that is working your body or that is working the universe. This body is being moved by a power of which will is only a manifestation in one part. Likewise in the universe there is will, but that is only one part of the universe. The whole of the universe is not guided by will; that is why we cannot explain it by the will theory. Suppose I take it for granted that it is will moving the body, then, when I find I cannot work it at will, I begin to fret and fume. It is my fault, because I had no right to take the will theory for granted. In the same way, if I take the universe and think it is will that moves it and find things which do not coincide, it is my fault. So the Purusha is not will; neither can it be intelligence, because intelligence itself is a compound. There cannot be any intelligence without some sort of matter corresponding to the brain. Wherever there is intelligence, there must be something akin to that matter which we call brain which becomes lumped together into a particular form and serves the purpose of the brain. Wherever there is intelligence, there must be that matter in some form or other. But intelligence itself is a compound. What then is this Purusha? It is neither intelligence nor will, but it is the cause of all these. It is its presence that sets them all going and combining. It does not mix with nature; it is not intelligence, or Mahat; but the Self, the pure, is Purusha. "I am the witness, and through my witnessing, nature is producing; all that is sentient and all that is insentient."

What is this sentiency in nature? We find intelligence is this sentiency which is called Chit. The basis of sentiency is in the Purusha, it is the nature of Purusha. It is that which cannot be explained but which is the cause of all that we call knowledge. Purusha is not consciousness, because consciousness is a compound; buts whatever is light and good in consciousness belongs to Purusha. Purusha is not conscious, but whatever is light in intelligence belongs to Purusha. Sentiency is in the Purusha, but the Purusha is not intelligent, not knowing. The Chit in the Purusha plus Prakriti is what we see around us. Whatever is pleasure and happiness and light in the universe belongs to Purusha; but it is a compound, because it is Purusha plus Prakriti. "Wherever there is any happiness, wherever there is any bliss, there is a spark of that immortality which is God." "Purusha is the; great attraction of the universe; though untouched by and unconnected with the universe, yet it attracts the whole; universe." You see a man going after gold, because behind it is a spark of the Purusha though mixed up with a good deal of dirt. When a man loves his children or a woman her husband, what is the attracting power? A spark of Purusha behind them. It is there, only mixed up with "dirt". Nothing else can attract. "In this world of insentiency the Purusha alone is sentient." This is the Purusha of the Sankhya. As such, it necessarily follows that the Purusha must be omnipresent. That which is not omnipresent must be limited. All limitations are caused; that which is caused must have a beginning and end. If the Purusha is limited, it will die, will not be free, will not be final, but must have some cause. Therefore it is omnipresent. According to Kapila, there are many Purushas; not one, but an infinite number of them. You and I have each of us one, and so has everyone else; an infinite number of circles, each one infinite, running through this universe. The Purusha is neither mind nor matter, the reflex from it is all that we know. We are sure if it is omnipresent it has neither death nor birth. Nature is casting her shadow upon it, the shadow of birth and death, but it is by its nature pure. So far we have found the philosophy of the Sankhya wonderful.

Next we shall take up the proofs against it. So far the analysis is perfect, the psychology incontrovertible. We find by the division of the senses into organs and instruments that they are not simple, but compound; by dividing egoism into sense and matter, we find that this is also material and that Mahat is also a state of matter, and finally we find the Purusha. So far there is no objection. But if we ask the Sankhya the question, "Who created nature?" — the Sankhya says that the Purusha and the Prakriti are uncreate and omnipresent, and that of this Purusha there is an infinite number. We shall have to controvert these propositions, and find a better solution, and by so doing we shall come to Advaitism. Our first objection is, how can there be these two infinites? Then our argument will be that the Sankhya is not a perfect generalization, and that we have not found in it a perfect solution. And then we shall see how the Vedantists grope out of all these difficulties and reach a perfect solution, and yet all the glory really belongs to the Sankhya. It is very easy to give a finishing touch to a building when it is constructed.

SANKHYA AND VEDANTA

I shall give you a résumé of the Sânkhya philosophy, through which we have been going. We, in this lecture, want to find where its defects are, and where Vedanta comes in and supplements it. You must remember that according to Sankhya philosophy, nature is the cause of all these manifestations which we call thought, intellect, reason, love, hatred, touch, taste, and matter. Everything is from nature. This nature consists of three sorts of elements, called Sattva, Rajas, and Tamas. These are not qualities, but elements, the materials out of which the whole universe is evolved. In the beginning of a cycle these remain in equilibrium; and when creation comes, they begin to combine and recombine and manifest as the universe. The first manifestation is what the Sankhya calls the Mahat or Intelligence, and out of that comes consciousness. According to Sankhya, this is an element (Tattva). And out of consciousness are evolved Manas or mind, the organs of the senses, and the Tanmâtras (particles of sound, touch, etc.). All the fine particles are evolved from consciousness, and out of these fine particles come the gross elements which we call matter. The Tanmatras cannot be perceived; but when they become gross particles, we can feel and sense them.

The Chitta, in its threefold function of intelligence, consciousness, and mind, works and manufactures the forces called Prâna. You must at once get rid of the idea that Prana is breath. Breath is one effect of Prana. By Prana are meant the nervous forces governing and moving the whole body, which also manifest themselves as thought. The foremost and most obvious manifestation of Prana is the breathing motion. Prana acts upon air, and not air upon it. Controlling the breathing motion is prânâyâma. Pranayama is practised to get mastery over this motion; the end is not merely to control the breath or to make the lungs strong. That is Delsarte, not Pranayama. These Pranas are the vital forces which manipulate the whole body, while they in their turn are manipulated by other organs in the body, which are called mind or internal organs. So far so good. The psychology is very clear and most precise; and yet it is the oldest rational thought in the world! Wherever there is any philosophy or rational thought, it owes something or other to Kapila. Pythagoras learnt it in India, and taught it in Greece. Later on Plato got an inkling of it; and still later the Gnostics carried the thought to Alexandria, and from there it came to Europe. So wherever there is any attempt at psychology or philosophy, the great father of it is this man, Kapila. So far we see that his psychology is wonderful; but we shall have to differ with him on some points, as we go on. We find that the basic principle on which Kapila works, is evolution. He makes one thing evolve out of another, because his very definition of causation is "the cause reproduced in another form," and because the whole universe, so far as we see it, is progressive and evolving. We see clay; in another form, we call it a pitcher. Clay was the cause and the pitcher the effect. Beyond this we cannot have any idea of causation. Thus this whole universe is evolved out of a material, out of Prakriti or nature. Therefore, the universe cannot be essentially different from its cause. According to Kapila, from undifferentiated nature to thought or intellect, not one of them is what he calls the "Enjoyer" or "Enlightener". Just as is a lump of clay, so is a lump of mind. By itself the mind has no light; but ate see it reasons. Therefore there must be some one behind it, whose light is percolating through Mahat and consciousness, and subsequent modifications, and this is what Kapila calls the Purusha, the Self of the Vedantin. According to Kapila, the Purusha is a simple entity, not a compound; he is immaterial, the only one who is immaterial, and all these various manifestations are material. I see a black-board. First, the external instruments will bring that sensation to the nerve-centre, to the Indriya according to Kapila; from the centre it will go to the mind and make an impression; the mind will present it to the Buddhi, but Buddhi cannot act; the action comes, as it were, from the Purusha behind. These, so to speak, are all his servants, bringing the sensations to him, and he, as it were, gives the orders, reacts, is the enjoyer, the perceiver, the real One, the King on his throne, the Self of man, who is immaterial. Because he is immaterial, it necessarily follows that he must be infinite, he cannot have any limitation whatever. Each one of the Purushas is omnipresent; each one of us is omnipresent, but we can act only through the Linga Sharira, the fine body. The mind, the self-consciousness, the organs, and the vital forces compose the fine body or sheath, what in Christian philosophy is called the spiritual body of man. It is this body that gets salvation, or punishment, or heaven, that incarnates and reincarnates, because we see from the very beginning that the going and the coming of the Purusha or soul are impossible. Motion means going or coming, and what goes or comes from one place to another cannot be omnipresent. Thus far we see from Kapila's psychology that the soul is infinite, and that the soul is the only thing which is not composed of nature. He is the only one that is outside of nature, but he has got bound by nature, apparently. Nature is around him, and he has identified himself with it. He thinks, "I am the Linga Sharira", "I am the gross matter, the gross body", and as such he enjoys pleasure and pain, but they do not really belong to him, they belong to this Linga Sharira or the fine body.

The meditative state is called always the highest state by the Yogi, when it is neither a passive nor an active state; in it you approach nearest to the Purusha. The soul has neither pleasure nor pain; it is the witness of everything, the eternal witness of all work, but it takes no fruits from any work. As the sun is the cause of sight of every eye, but is not itself affected by any defects in the eye or as when a crystal has red or blue flowers placed before it, the crystal looks red or blue, and yet it is neither; so, the soul is neither passive nor active, it is beyond both. The nearest way of expressing this state of the soul is that it is meditation. This is Sankhya philosophy.

Next, Sankhya says, that the manifestation of nature is for the soul; all combinations are for some third person. The combinations which you call nature, these constant changes are going on for the enjoyment of the soul, for its liberation, that it may gain all this experience from the lowest to the highest. When it has gained it, the soul finds it was never in nature, that it was entirely separate, that it is indestructible, that it cannot go and come; that going to heaven and being born again were in nature, and not in the soul. Thus the soul becomes free. All nature is working for the enjoyment and experience of the soul. It is getting this experience in order to reach the goal, and that goal is freedom. But the souls are many according to the Sankhya philosophy. There is an infinite number of souls. The other conclusion of Kapila is that there is no God as the Creator of the universe. Nature is quite sufficient by itself to account for everything. God is not necessary, says the Sankhya.

The Vedanta says that the Soul is in its nature Existence absolute, Knowledge absolute, Bliss absolute. But these are not qualities of the Soul: they are one, not three, the essence of the Soul; and it agrees with the Sankhya in thinking that intelligence belongs to nature, inasmuch as it comes through nature. The Vedanta also shows that what is called intelligence is a compound. For instance, let us examine our perceptions. I see a black-board. How does the knowledge come? What the German philosophers call "the thing-in-itself" of the blackboard is unknown, I can never know it. Let us call it x . The black-board x acts on my mind, and the mind reacts. The mind is like a lake. Throw a stone in a lake and a reactionary wave comes towards the stone; this wave is not like the stone at all, it is a wave. The black-board x is like a stone which strikes the mind and the mind throws up a wave towards it, and this wave is what we call the black-board. I see you. You as reality are unknown and unknowable. You are x and you act upon my mind, and the mind throws a wave in the direction from which the impact comes, and that wave is what I call Mr. or Mrs. So-and-so. There are two elements in the perception, one coming from outside and the other from inside, and the combination of these two, x + mind, is our external universe. All knowledge is by reaction. In the case of a whale it has been determined by calculation how long after its tail is struck, its mind reacts and the whale feels the pain. Similar is the case with internal perception. The real self within me is also unknown and unknowable.

Let us call it y . When I know myself as so-and-so, it is y + the mind. That y strikes a blow on the mind. So our whole world is x + mind (external), and y + mind (internal), x and y standing for the thing-in-itself behind the external and the internal worlds respectively.

According to Vedanta, the three fundamental factors of consciousness are, I exist, I know, and I am blessed The idea that I have no want, that I am restful, peaceful, that nothing can disturb me, which comes from time to time, is the central fact of our being, the basic principle of our life; and when it becomes limited, and becomes a compound, it manifests itself as existence phenomenal, knowledge phenomenal, and love. Every man exists, and every man must know, and every man is mad for love. He cannot help loving. Through all existence, from the lowest to the highest, all must love. The y , the internal thing-in-itself, which, combining with mind, manufactures existence, knowledge, and love, is called by the Vedantists. Existence absolute, Knowledge absolute, Bliss absolute. That real existence is limitless, unmixed, uncombined, knows no change, is the free soul; when it gets mixed up, muddled up, as it were, with the mind, it becomes what we call individual existence. It is plant life, animal life, human life, just as universal space is cut off in a room, in a jar, and so on. And that real knowledge is not what we know, not intuition, nor reason, nor instinct. When that degenerates and is confused, we call it intuition; when it degenerates more, we call it reason; and when it degenerates still more, we call it instinct. That knowledge itself is Vijnâna, neither intuition, nor reason nor instinct. The nearest expression for it is all-knowingness. There is no limit to it, no combination in it. That bliss, when it gets clouded over, we call love, attraction for gross bodies or fine bodies, or for ideas. This is only a distorted manifestation of that blessedness. Absolute Existence, absolute Knowledge, and absolute Blessedness are not qualities of the soul, but the essence; there is no difference between them and the soul. And the three are one; we see the one thing in three different aspects. They are beyond all relative knowledge. That eternal knowledge of the Self percolating through the brain of man becomes his intuition, reason, and so on. Its manifestation varies according to the medium through which it shines. As soul, there is no difference between man and the lowest animal, only the latter's brain is less developed and the manifestation through it which we call instinct is very dull. In a man the brain is much finer, so the manifestation is much clearer, and in the highest man it becomes entirely clear. So with existence; the existence which we know, the limited sphere of existence, is simply a reflection of that real existence which is the nature of the soul. So with bliss; that which we call love or attraction is but the rejection of the eternal blessedness of the Self. With manifestation comes limitation, but the unmanifested, the essential nature of the soul, is unlimited; to that blessedness there is no limit. But in love there is limitation. I love you one day, I hate you the next. My love increases one day and decreases the next, because it is only a manifestation.

The first point we will contend with Kapila is his idea of God. Just as the series of modifications of Prakriti, beginning with the individual intellect and ending with the individual body, require a Purusha behind, as the ruler and governor, so, in the Cosmos, the universal intellect, the universal egoism, the universal mind, all

universal fine and gross materials, must have a ruler and governor. How will the cosmic series become complete without the universal Purusha behind them all as the ruler and governor? If you deny a universal Purusha behind the cosmic series, we deny your Purusha behind the individual series. If it be true that behind the series of graded, evolved individual manifestations, there stands One that is beyond them all, the Purusha who is not composed of matter, the very same logic will apply to the case of universal manifestations. This Universal Self which is beyond the universal modifications of Prakriti is what is called Ishwara, the Supreme Ruler, God.

Now comes the more important point of difference. Can there be more than one Purusha? The Purusha, we have seen, is omnipresent and infinite. The omnipresent, the infinite, cannot be two. If there are two infinites A and B, the infinite A would limit the infinite B, because the infinite B is not the infinite A, and the infinite A is not the infinite B. Difference in identity means exclusion, and exclusion means limitation. Therefore, A and B, limiting each other, cease to be infinites. Hence, there can be but one infinite, that is, one Purusha.

Now we will take up our x and y and show they are one. We have shown how what we call the external world is x + mind, and the internal world y + mind; x and y are both quantities unknown and unknowable. All difference is due to time, space, and causation. These are the constituent elements of the mind. No mentality is possible without them. You can never think without time, you can never imagine anything without space, and you can never have anything without causation. These are the forms of the mind. Take them away, and the mind itself does not exist.

All difference is, therefore, due to the mind. According to Vedanta, it is the mind, its forms, that have limited x and y apparently and made them appear as external and internal worlds. But x and y , being both beyond the mind, are without difference and hence one. We cannot attribute any quality to them, because qualities are born of the mind. That which is qualityless must be one; x is without qualities, it only takes qualities of the mind; so does y ; therefore these x and y are one. The whole universe is one. There is only one Self in the universe, only One Existence, and that One Existence, when it passes through the forms of time, space, and causation, is called by different names, Buddhi, fine matter, gross matter, all mental and physical forms. Everything in the universe is that One, appearing in various forms. When a little part of it comes, as it were, into this network of time, space, and causation, it takes forms; take off the network, and it is all one. Therefore in the Advaita philosophy, the whole universe is all one in the Self which is called Brahman. That Self when it appears behind the universe is called God. The same Self when it appears behind this little universe, the body, is the soul. This very soul, therefore, is the Self in man. There is only one Purusha, the Brahman of the Vedanta; God and man, analysed, are one in It. The universe is you yourself, the unbroken you; you are throughout the universe. "In all hands you work, through all mouths you eat, through all nostrils you breathe through all minds you think." The whole universe is you; the universe is your body; you are the universe both formed and unformed. You are the soul of the universe and its body also. You are God, you are the angels, you are man, you are animals, you are the plants, you are the minerals, you are everything; the manifestation of everything is you. Whatever exists is you. You are the Infinite. The Infinite cannot be divided.

It can have no parts, for each part would be infinite, and then the part would be identical with the whole, which is absurd. Therefore the idea that you are Mr. So-and-so can never be true; it is a day-dream. Know this and be free. This is the Advaita conclusion. "I am neither the body, nor the organs, nor am I the mind; I am Existence, Knowledge, and Bliss absolute; I am He." This is true knowledge; all reason and intellect, and everything else is ignorance. Where is knowledge for me, for I am knowledge itself! Where is life for me, for I am life itself! I am sure I live, for I am life, the One Being, and nothing exists except through me, and in me, and as me. I am manifested through the elements, but I am the free One. Who seeks freedom? Nobody. If you think that you are bound, you remain bound; you make your own bondage. If you know that you are free, you are free this moment. This is knowledge, knowledge of freedom. Freedom is the goal of all nature.

THE GOAL

(Delivered in San Francisco, March 27, 1900)

(Reprinted from the Vedanta and the West , May-June 1958. The editors of the Magazine published it as it was recorded, adding certain words (in square brackets) to maintain the continuity of thought, and periods to indicate omissions that might have occurred in recording. — Ed.)

We find that man, as it were, is always surrounded by something greater than himself, and he is trying to grasp the meaning of this. Man will ever [seek] the highest ideal. He knows that it exists and that religion is the search after the highest ideal. At first all his searches were in the external plane — placed in heaven, in different places — just according to [his grasp] of the total nature of man.

[Later,] man began to look at himself a little closer and began to find out that the real "me" was not the "me" that he stands for ordinarily. As he appears to the senses is not the same as he really is. He began to [search] inside of himself, and found out that . . . the same ideal he [had placed] outside of himself is all the time within; what he was worshipping outside was his own real inner nature. The difference between dualism and monism is that when the ideal is put outside [of oneself], it is dualism. When God is [sought] within, it is monism.

First, the old question of why and wherefore . . . How is it that man became limited? How did the Infinite become finite, the pure become impure? In the first place, you must never forget that this question can never be answered [by] any dualistic hypothesis.

Why did God create the impure universe? Why is man so miserable, made by a perfect, infinite, merciful Father? Why this heaven and earth, looking at which we get our conception of law? Nobody can imagine anything that he has not seen.

All the tortures we feel in this life, we put in another place and that is our hell . . . .

Why did the infinite God make this world? [The dualist says:] Just as the potter makes pots. God the potter; we the pots. . . . In more philosophical language the question is: How is it taken for granted that the real nature of man is pure, perfect, and infinite? This is the one difficulty found in any system of monism. Everything else is clean and clear. This question cannot be answered. The monists say the question itself is a contradiction.

Take the system of dualism — the question is asked why God created the world. This is contradictory. Why? Because — what is the idea of God? He is a being who cannot be acted upon by anything outside.

You and I are not free. I am thirsty. There is something called thirst, over which I have no control, [which] forces me to drink water. Every action of my body and even every thought of my mind is forced out of me. I have got to do it. That is why I am bound . . . . I am forced to do this, to have this, and so on . . . . And what is meant by why and wherefore? [Being subject to external forces.] Why do you drink water? Because thirst forces you. You are a slave. You never do anything of your own will because you are forced to do everything. Your only motive for action is some force. . . .

The earth, by itself, would never move unless something forced it. Why does the light burn? It does not burn unless somebody comes and strikes a match. Throughout nature, everything is bound. Slavery, slavery! To be in harmony with nature is [slavery]. What is there in being the slave of nature and living in a golden cage? The greatest law and order is in the [knowledge that man is essentially free and divine] Now we see that the question why and wherefore can only be asked [in ignorance]. I can only be forced to do something through something else.

[You say] God is free. Again you ask the question why God creates the world. You contradict yourself. The meaning of God is entirely free will. The question put in logical language is this: What forced Him, who can never be forced by anybody, to create the world? You say in the same question, What forced Him? The question is nonsense. He is infinite by His very nature; He is free. We shall answer questions when you can ask them in logical language. Reason will tell you that there is only one Reality, nothing else. Wherever dualism has risen, monism came to a head and drove it out.

There is only one difficulty in understanding this. Religion is a common-sense, everyday thing. The man in the street knows it if you put it in his language and not [if it is put] in a philosopher's language. It is a common thing in human nature to [project itself]. Think of your feeling with the child. [You identify yourself with it. Then] you have two bodies. [Similarly] you can feel through your husband's mind Where can you stop? You can feel in infinite bodies.

Nature is conquered by man every day. As a race, man is manifesting his power. Try in imagination to put a limit to this power in man. You admit that man as a race has infinite power, has [an] infinite body. The only question is what you are. Are you the race or one [individual]? The moment you isolate yourself, everything hurts you. The moment you expand and feel for others, you gain help. The selfish man is the most miserable in the world. The happiest is the man who is not at all selfish. He has become the whole creation, the whole race and God [is] within him. . . . So in dualism — Christian, Hindu, and all religions — the code of ethics . . . . is: Do not be selfish . . . . things for others! Expand! . . . .

The ignorant can be made to understand [this] very easily, and the learned can be made to understand still more easily. But the man who has just got a speck of learning, him God himself cannot make understand. [The truth is,] you are not separate [from this universe]; Just as your Spirit] is [not] separate from the rest of you. If [not] so, you could not see anything, could not feel anything. Our bodies are simply little whirlpools in the ocean of matter. Life is taking a turn and passing on, in another form . . . . The sun, the moon, the stars, you and I are mere whirlpools. Why did I select [a particular mind as mine? It is] simply a mental whirlpool in the ocean of mind.

How else is it possible that my vibration reaches you just now? If you throw a stone in the lake, it raises a vibration and [that stirs] the water into vibration. I throw my mind into the state of bliss and the tendency is to raise the same bliss in your mind. How often in your mind or heart [you have thought something] and without [verbal] communication, [others have got your thought]? Everywhere we are one. . . . That is what we never understand. The whole [universe] is composed of time, space, and causation. And God [appears as this universe]. . . . When did nature begin? When you [forgot your true nature and] became [bound by time, space, and causation].

This is the [rotating] circle of your bodies and yet that is your infinite nature. . . . That is certainly nature — time, space, and causation. That is all that is meant by nature. Time began when you began to think. Space began when you got the body; otherwise there cannot be any space. Causation began when you became limited. We have to have some sort of answer. There is the answer. [Our limitation] is play. Just for the fun of it. Nothing binds you; nothing forces [you. You were] never bound. We are all acting our parts in this [play] of our own invention.

But let us bring another question about individuality. Some people are so afraid of losing their individuality. Wouldn't it be better for the pig to lose his pig-individuality if he can become God? Yes. But the poor pig does not think so at the time. Which state is my individuality? When I was a baby sprawling on the floor trying to swallow my thumb? Was that the individuality I should be sorry to lose? Fifty years hence I shall look upon this present state and laugh, just as I [now] look upon the baby state. Which of these individualities shall I keep ? . . .

We are to understand what is meant by this individuality. . . . [There are two opposite tendencies:] one is the protection of the individuality, the other is the intense desire to sacrifice the individuality. . . . The mother sacrifices all her own will for the needy baby. . . . When she carries the baby in her arms, the call of individuality, of self-preservation is no more heard. She will eat the worst food, but her children will have the best. So for all the people we love we are ready to die.

[On the one hand] we are struggling hard to keep up this individuality; on the other hand, trying to kill it. With what result? Tom Brown may struggle hard. He is [fighting] for his individuality. Tom dies and there is not a ripple anywhere upon the surface of the earth. There was a Jew born nineteen hundred years ago, and he never moved a finger to keep his individuality. . . . Think of that! That Jew never struggled to protect his individuality. That is why he became the greatest in the world. This is what the world does not know.

In time we are to be individuals. But in what sense? What is the individuality of man? Not Tom Brown, but God in man. That is the [true] individuality. The more man has approached that, the more he has given up his false individuality. The more he tries to collect and gain

everything [for himself], the less he is an individual. The less he has thought of [himself], the more he has sacrificed all individuality during his lifetime, . . . the more he is an individual. This is one secret the world does not understand.

We must first understand what is meant by individuality. It is attaining the ideal. You are man now, [or] you are woman. You will change all the time. Can you stop? Do you want to keep your minds as they are now — the angels, hatreds, jealousies, quarrels, all the thousand and one things in the mind? Do you mean to say that you will keep them? . . . You cannot stop anywhere . . . until perfect conquest has been achieved, until you are pure and you are perfect.

You have no more anger when you are all love, bliss, infinite existence. . . . Which of your bodies will you keep? You cannot stop anywhere until you come to life that never ends. Infinite life! You stop there. You have a little knowledge now and are always trying to get more. Where will you stop? Nowhere, until you become one with life itself. . . .

Many want pleasure [as] the goal. For that pleasure they seek only the senses. On the higher planes much pleasure is to be sought. Then on spiritual planes. Then in himself — God within him. The man whose pleasure is outside of [himself] becomes unhappy when that outside thing goes. You cannot depend for this pleasure upon anything in this universe. If all my pleasures are in myself, I must have pleasure there all the time because I can never lose my Self. . . . Mother, father, child, wife, body, wealth

— everything I can lose except my self . . . bliss in the Self All desire is contained in the Self. . . . This. is individuality which never changes, and this is perfect.

. . . And how to get it? They find what the great souls of this world — all great men and women — found [through sustained discrimination]. . . . What of these dualistic theories of twenty gods, thirty gods? It does not matter. They all had the one truth, that this false individuality must go. . . . So this ego — the less there is of it, the nearer I am to that which I really am: the universal body. The less I think of my own individual mind, the nearer I am to that universal mind. The less I think of my own soul, the nearer I am to the universal soul.

We live in one body. We have some pain, some pleasure. Just for this little pleasure we have by living in this body, we are ready to kill everything in the universe to preserve ourselves. If we had two bodies. would not that be much better? So on and on to bliss. I am in everybody. Through all hands I work; through all feet I walk. I speak through every mouth; I live in every body. Infinite my bodies, infinite my minds. I lived in Jesus of Nazareth, in Buddha, in Mohammed — in all the great and good of the past, of the present. I am going to live in all that [may] come afterwards. Is that theory [No, it is the truth.]

If you can realise this, how infinitely more pleasurable that will be. What an ecstasy of joy! Which one body is so great that we need here anything [of] the body. . . After living in all the bodies of others, all the bodies there are in this world, what becomes of us? [We become one with the Infinite. And] that is the goal. That is the only way. One [man] says, "If I know the truth, I shall be melted away like butter." I wish people would be, but they are too tough to be melted so quickly!

What are we to do to be free? Free you are already. . . . How could the free ever be bound? It is a lie. [You were] never bound. How could the unlimited ever be limited by anything? Infinite divided by infinite, added to infinite, multiplied by infinite [remains] infinite. You are infinite; God is infinite. You are all infinite. There cannot be two existences, only one. The Infinite can never be made finite. You are never bound. That is all. . . . You are free already. You have reached the goal — all there is to reach. Never allow the mind to think that you have not reached the goal. . . .

Whatever we [think] that we become. If you think you are poor sinners you hypnotise yourselves: "I am a miserable, crawling worm." Those who believe in hell are in hell when they die; those who say that they will go to heaven [go to heaven].

It is all play. . . . [You may say,] "We have to do something; let us do good." [But] who cares for good and evil? Play! God Almighty plays. That is all. . . .You are the almighty God playing. If you want to play on the side and take the part of a beggar, you are not [to blame someone else for making that choice]. You enjoy being the beggar. You know your real nature [to be divine]. You are the king and play you are a beggar. . . . It is all fun. Know it and play. That is all there is to it. Then practice it. The whole universe is a vast play. All is good because all is fun. This star comes and crashes with our earth, and we are

all dead. [That too is fun.] You only think fun the little things that delight your senses! . . .

[We are told that there is] one good god here, and one bad god there always on the watch to grab me the moment I make a mistake. . . . When I was a child I was told by someone that God watches everything. I went to bed and looked up and expected the ceiling of the room to open. [Nothing happened.] Nobody is watching us except ourselves. No Lord except our [own Self]; no nature but what we feel. Habit is second nature; it is first nature also. It is all there is of nature. I repeat [something] two or three times; it becomes my nature. Do not be miserable! Do not repent! What is done is done. If you burn yourself, [take the consequences].

. . . Be sensible. We make mistakes; what of that? That is all in fun. They go so crazy over their past sins, moaning and weeping and all that. Do not repent! After having done work, do not think of it. Go on! Stop not! Don't look back! What will you gain by looking back? You lose nothing, gain nothing. You are not going to be melted like butter. Heavens and hells and incarnations — all nonsense!

Who is born and who dies? You are having fun, playing with worlds and all that. You keep this body as long as you like. If you do not like it, do not have it. The Infinite is the real; the finite is the play. You are the infinite body and the finite body in one. Know it! But knowledge will not make any difference; the play will go on. . . . Two words — soul and body — have been joined. [Partial] knowledge is the cause. Know that you are always free.

The fire of knowledge burns down all the [impurities and limitations]. I am that Infinite. . . .

You are as free as you were in the beginning, are now, and always will be. He who knows that he is free is free; he who knows that he is bound is bound.

What becomes of God and worship and all that? They have their place. I have divided myself into God and me; I become the worshipped and I worship myself. Why not? God is I. Why not worship my Self? The universal God — He is also my Self. It is all fun. There is no other purpose.

What is the end and aim of life? None, because I [know that I am the Infinite]. If you are beggars, you can have aims. I have no aims, no want, no purpose. I come to your country, and lecture — just for fun. No other meaning. What meaning can be there? Only slaves do actions for somebody else. You do actions for nobody else. When it suits you, you worship. You can join the Christians, the Mohammedans, the Chinese, the Japanese. You can worship all the gods that ever were and are ever going to be. . . .

I am in the sun, the moon, and the stars. I am with God and I am in all the gods. I worship my Self.

There is another side to it. I have kept it in reserve. I am the man that is going to be hanged. I am all the wicked. I am getting punished in hells. That [also] is fun. This is the goal of philosophy [to know that I am the Infinite]. Aims, motives, purposes, and duties live in the background. . . .

This truth is first to be listened to then to be thought about. Reason, argue it out by all manner of means. The enlightened know no more than that. Know it for certain that you are in everything. That is why you should not hurt anybody, because in hurting them you hurt yourself. . . . [Lastly,] this is to be meditated upon. Think upon it. Can you realise there will come a time when everything will crumble in the dust and you will stand alone? That moment of ecstatic joy will never leave you. You will actually find that you are without bodies. You never had bodies.

I am One, alone, through all eternity. Whom shall I fear? It is all my Self. This is continuously to be meditated upon. Through that comes realisation. It is through realisation that you become a [blessing] to others. . . .

"Thy face shines like [that of] one who has known God." (Chhândogya. IV. ix. That is the goal. This is not to be preached as I am doing. "Under a tree I saw a teacher, a boy of sixteen; the disciple was an old man of eighty. The teacher was teaching in silence, and the doubts of the disciple vanished." (Dakshinâmurtistotram , 1 And who speaks? Who lights a candle to see the sun? When the truth [dawns], no witness is necessary. You know it . . . . That is what you are going to do: . . . realise it. [first think of it. Reason it out. Satisfy your curiosity. Then [think] of nothing else. I wish we never read anything. Lord help us all! Just see what [a learned] man becomes.

"This is said, and that is said. . . ."

"What do you say, my friend?"

"I say nothing." [He quotes] everybody else's thought; but he thinks nothing. If this is education, what is lunacy? Look at all the men who wrote! . . . These modern writers, not two sentences their own! All quotations. . . .

There is not much value in books, and in [secondhand] religion there is no value whatsoever. It is like eating. Your religion would not satisfy me Jesus saw God and Buddha saw God. If you have not seen God, you are no better than the atheist. Only he is quiet, and you talk much and disturb the world with your talk. Books and bibles and scriptures are of no use. I met an old man when I was a boy; [he did not study any scripture, but he transmitted the truth of God by a touch].

Silence ye teachers of the world. Silence ye books. Lord, Thou alone speak and Thy servant listeneth. . . . If truth is not there, what is the use of this life? We all think we will catch it, but we do not. Most of us catch only dust. God is not there. If no God, what is the use of life? Is there any resting-place in the universe? [It is up to us to find it]; only we do not [search for it intensely. We are] like a little piece of maw carried on in the current.

If there is this truth, if there is God, it must be within us. . . . [I must be able to say,] "I have seen Him with my eyes," Otherwise I have no religion. Beliefs, doctrines, sermons do not make religion. It is realisation, perception of God [which alone is religion]. What is the glory of all these men whom the world worships? God was no more a doctrine [for them. Did they believe] because their grandfather believed it? No. It was the realisation of the Infinite, higher than their own bodies, minds, and everything. This world is real inasmuch as it contains a little bit [of] the reflection of that God. We love the good man because in his face shines the reflection a little more. We must catch it ourselves. There is no other way.

That is the goal. Struggle for it! Have your own Bible. Have your own Christ. Otherwise you are not religious. Do not talk religion. Men talk and talk. “Some of them, steeped in darkness, in the pride of their hearts think that they have the light. And not only [that], they offer to take others upon their shoulders and both fall into the pit.” (Katha, I. ii. . . .

No church ever saved by itself. It is good to be born in a temple, but woe unto the person who dies in a temple or church. Out of it! . . . It was a good beginning, but leave it! It was the childhood place . . . but let it be! . . . Go to God directly. No theories, no doctrines. Then alone will all doubts vanish. Then alone will all crookedness be made straight. . . .

In the midst of the manifold, he who sees that One; in the midst of this infinite death, he who sees that one life; in the midst of the manifold, he who sees that which never changes in his own soul — unto him belongs eternal peace.

Unity, the Goal of Religion

(Delivered in New York, 1896)

This universe of ours, the universe of the senses, the rational, the intellectual, is bounded on both sides by the illimitable, the unknowable, the ever unknown. Herein is the search, herein are the inquiries, here are the facts; from this comes the light which is known to the world as religion. Essentially, however, religion belongs to the supersensuous and not to the sense plane. It is beyond all reasoning and is not on the plane of intellect. It is a vision, an inspiration, a plunge into the unknown and unknowable, making the unknowable more than known for it can never be "known". This search has been in the human mind, as I believe, from the very beginning of humanity. There cannot have been human reasoning and intellect in any period of the world's history without this struggle, this search beyond. In our little universe, this human mind, we see a thought arise. Whence it arises we do not know; and when it disappears, where it goes, we know not either. The macrocosm and the microcosm are, as it were, in the same groove, passing through the same stages, vibrating in the same key.

I shall try to bring before you the Hindu theory that religions do not come from without, but from within. It is my belief that religious thought is in man's very constitution, so much so that it is impossible for him to give, up religion until he can give up his mind and body, until he can give up thought and life. As long as a man thinks, this struggle must go on, and so long man must have some form of religion. Thus we see various forms of religion in the world. It is a bewildering study; but it is not, as many of us think, a vain speculation. Amidst this chaos there is harmony, throughout these discordant sounds there is a note of concord; and he who is prepared to listen to it will catch the tone.

The great question of all questions at the present time is this: Taking for granted that the known and the knowable are bounded on both sides by the unknowable and the infinitely unknown, why struggle for that infinite unknown? Why shall we not be content with the known? Why shall we not rest satisfied with eating, drinking, and doing a little good to society? This idea is in the air. From the most learned professor to the prattling baby, we are told that to do good to the world is all of religion, and that it is useless to trouble ourselves about questions of the beyond. So much is this the case that it has become a truism.

But fortunately we must inquire into the beyond. This present, this expressed, is only one part of that unexpressed. The sense universe is, as it were, only one portion, one bit of that infinite spiritual universe projected into the plane of sense consciousness. How can this little bit of projection be explained, be understood, without. knowing that which is beyond? It is said of Socrates that one day while lecturing at Athens, he met a Brahmin who had travelled into Greece, and Socrates told the Brahmin that the greatest study for mankind is man. The Brahmin sharply retorted: "How can you know man until you know Gods" This God, this eternally Unknowable, or Absolute, or Infinite, or without name — you may call Him by what name you like — is the rationale, the only explanation, the raison d'être of that which is known and knowable, this present life. Take anything before you, the most material thing — take one of the most material sciences, as chemistry or physics, astronomy or biology — study it, push the study forward and forward, and the gross forms will begin to melt and become finer and finer, until they come to a point where you are bound to make a tremendous leap from these material things into the immaterial. The gross melts into the fine, physics into metaphysics, in every department of knowledge.

Thus man finds himself driven to a study of the beyond. Life will be a desert, human life will be vain, if we cannot know the beyond. It is very well to say: Be contented with the things of the present. The cows and the dogs are, and so are all animals; and that is what makes them animals. So if man rests content with the present and gives up all search into the beyond, mankind will have to go back to the animal plane again. It is religion, the inquiry into the beyond, that makes the difference between man and an animal. Well has it been said that man is the only animal that naturally looks upwards; every other animal naturally looks down. That looking upward and going upward and seeking perfection are what is called salvation; and the sooner a man begins to go higher, the sooner he raises himself towards this idea of truth as salvation. It does not consist in the amount of money in your pocket, or the dress you wear, or the house you live in, but in the wealth of spiritual thought in your brain. That is what makes for human progress, that is the source of all material and intellectual progress, the motive power behind, the enthusiasm that pushes mankind forward.

Religion does not live on bread, does not dwell in a house. Again and again you hear this objection advanced: "What good can religion do? Can it take away the poverty of the poor?" Supposing it cannot, would that prove the untruth of religion? Suppose a baby stands up among you when you are trying to demonstrate an astronomical theorem, and says, "Does it bring gingerbread?" "No, it does not", you answer. "Then," says the baby, "it is useless." Babies judge the whole universe from their own standpoint, that of producing gingerbread, and so do the babies of the world. We must not judge of higher things from a low standpoint. Everything must be judged by its own standard and the infinite must be judged by the standard of infinity. Religion permeates the whole of man's life, not only the present, but the past, present, and future. It is, therefore, the eternal relation between the eternal soul and the eternal God. Is it logical to measure its value by its action upon five minutes of human life? Certainly not. These are all negative arguments.

Now comes the question: Can religion really accomplish anything? It can. It brings to man eternal life. It has made man what he is, and will make of this human animal a god. That is what religion can do. Take religion from human society and what will remain? Nothing but a forest of brutes. Sense-happiness is not the goal of humanity. Wisdom (Jnâna) is the goal of all life. We find that man enjoys his intellect more than an animal enjoys its senses; and we see that man enjoys his spiritual nature even more than his rational nature. So the highest wisdom must be this spiritual knowledge. With this knowledge will come bliss. All these things of this world are but the shadows, the manifestations in the third or fourth degree of the real Knowledge and Bliss.

One question more: What is the goal? Nowadays it is asserted that man is infinitely progressing, forward and forward, and there is no goal of perfection to attain to. Ever approaching, never attaining, whatever that may mean and however wonderful it may be, it is absurd on the face of it. Is there any motion in a straight line? A straight line infinitely projected becomes a circle, it returns to the starting point. You must end where you begin; and as you began in God, you must go back to God. What remains? Detail work. Through eternity you have to do the detail work.

Yet another question: Are we to discover new truths of religion as we go on? Yea and nay. In the first place, we cannot know anything more of religion, it has all been known. In all religions of the world you will find it claimed that there is a unity within us. Being one with divinity, there cannot be any further progress in that sense. Knowledge means finding this unity. I see you as men and women, and this is variety. It becomes scientific knowledge when I group you together and call you human beings. Take the science of chemistry, for instance. Chemists are seeking to resolve all known substances into their original elements, and if possible, to find the one element from which all these are derived. The time may come when they will find one element that is the source of all other elements. Reaching that, they can go no further; the science of chemistry will have become perfect. So it is with the science of religion. If we can discover this perfect unity, there cannot be any further progress.

The next question is: Can such a unity be found? In India the attempt has been made from the earliest times to reach a science of religion and philosophy, for the Hindus do not separate these as is customary in Western countries. We regard religion and philosophy as but two aspects of one thing which must equally be grounded in reason and scientific truth.

The system of the Sânkhya philosophy is one of the most ancient in India, or in fact in the world. Its great exponent Kapila is the father of all Hindu psychology; and the ancient system that he taught is still the foundation of all accepted systems of philosophy in India today which are known as the Darshanas. They all adopt his psychology, however widely they differ in other respects.

The Vedanta, as the logical outcome of the Sankhya, pushes its conclusions yet further. While its cosmology agrees with that taught by Kapila, the Vedanta is not satisfied to end in dualism, but continues its search for the final unity which is alike the goal of science and religion.

The mission of the Institute of Thought and Philosophy is to preserve and propagate the teachings of Swami Vivekananda. This great Indian spiritual leader is known for introducing the West to Hinduism. Drawing from his vast literary legacy, we provide valuable insights and practical guidance for modern living.

Have any query or feedback? Please reach out to us at

ITPPress123@gmail.com